Only When I Laugh

Only When I Laugh

Elouise Bell

SIGNATURE BOOKS
SALT LAKE CITY
1990

The majority of these essays originally appeared in *Network* magazine.

Cover Photograph: Jack McManemin

Cover Design: Julie Easton

94   93   92   91   90   6   5   4   3   2   1

LIBRARY OF CONGRESS CATALOGING-IN-PUBLICATION DATA

Bell,Elouise M.
   Only when I laugh / Elouise M. Bell.
    p. cm.
   1-56085-013-2 : $9.95
   I. Title.
PN4838.B45 1990
814'.54—dc20   90-48786
                                                     CIP

CONTENTS

ONE

Zzzzzucchini

It's amazing how often the simple truth in a cause-and-effect relationship is missed by an otherwise intelligent observer. For instance, a few years ago, the makers of Postum and Sanka looked into their sales reports and found an amazing peak in the Utah area. Excited by how well their products were doing, they sent a research analyst, with a well-cushioned expense account, to Utah with instructions to put in six weeks research time in order to discover why the Beehivers bought so much Postum and Sanka. I've always been curious as to what the analyst did for the five weeks and six days after finding the answer. Maybe fortune smiled, and the assignment came during ski season.

All this is by way of admitting that I have just recently come to understand why there are so many zucchini recipes in the world, and especially in this part of the world. Just the other day I saw a pamphlet claiming to offer one hundred recipes for zucchini.

Now, we don't have green bean cookbooks, do we? Or "One Hundred Wonderful Ways with Watermelon"? We don't have recipes for radish bread, or celery cake or cucumber soup. (Yes, I believe there is such a thing, but no one carries on about it.)

You see, that was what stumped me—the way people carried on about the recipes. I have friends who greet the announcement of a new zucchini recipe with a great deal more excitement than they gave to the discovery of cold fusion. What am I saying? I know newborn babies who don't get the welcome a new zucchini recipe gets!

And, until recently, this reception always puzzled me. Did other people really find this nondescript little vegetable all that delicious, that they were ever on the watch for new and better ways to serve it? Was it really such ambrosia to them that they couldn't get enough of the stuff, and vied with each other for more and more imaginative concoctions? ("Look: zucchini waffles! Hey—have you tried homemade zucchini ice cream yet? Listen, take my word for it: zucchini-oyster dip is terrific!")

In a way, it was like being color-blind. Apparently, everybody else in the world was seeing, or in this case tasting, something that just didn't come through to me. I didn't especially dislike the stuff, but I was not about to vote for it to replace chocolate chocolate-chip as the All-American dish.

And then, as I was sitting in my office one day, gazing pensively (or perhaps just groggily) out the window at majestic Timpanogos, the whole Truth came into my mind, all of one piece, as the Theory of Gravity came to Newton.

Eureka! There are so many zucchini recipes because . . . there is so much zucchini!

And why is there so much zucchini? Because apparently, zucchini crops never fail. I hear tales of people running out on frosty nights to cover up their tomatoes, tales of fruit farmers burning smudge pots to protect the apricots or peaches. I see people planting marigold borders around the vegetable garden to ward off the corn borer. But nobody seems to lose a wink of sleep over the zucchini: it seems to be the weed of the vegetable world.

I may have told you about my non-gardening but devout Mormon friend who finally decided she should follow the counsel of church leaders and put in a garden. She tore up a portion of her plush backyard, tilled and harrowed, and then put in four rows of zucchini. Four rows. Long ones. Of zucchini. When, in the fall, she began showing up at our meetings with dark circles under her eyes, I asked about it. Seems she had been getting very little sleep since harvest time. Instead, she was making nightly forays, out in ever-widening circles, to deposit bushel baskets of zucchini (with a few tomatoes on top as window dressing) on doorsteps of neighbors, ward members, stake members, neighbors of relatives, relatives of neighbors . . . Last thing I heard, she was doing a midnight shuttle out Wendover way.

Why do people climb mountains? Because they are there, we're told. And why do people plant zucchini? Because it grows. And because it grows so abundantly, people in this region will sell the family water rights to find yet one more way to use the stuff up!

But I've heard of a group of women in east Salt Lake who may have licked the whole problem once and for all. It seems they have discovered a method of laminating zucchini. Do the possibilities ripple out before you? Zucchini coasters? Zucchini napkin rings? Zucchini playing cards? (That'd solve the face-card dilemma permanently for card-loving Mormons and bring an end to the nuisance of playing pinochle with Rook cards.) Zucchini ear-rings? Bracelets? Zucchini campaign buttons? Zucchini picture frames?

Why, we haven't even tapped the possibilities yet! Don't give up the zucchini!

TWO

The Mug-wump

In the struggle for the advancement of any cause, no one is a more popular target than the fence-sitter. Even so, the position of the mug-wump, while never a comfortable one, may frequently be valid. ("Mug-wump," incidentally, was a nineteenth-century coinage for the person who sat with "mug" on one side of the fence and "wump" on the other.)

Being a fence-sitter is especially difficult in Utah, for surely no state in the Union has quite as many armed camps as we do, complete with dividing fences.

Of course, the fact is that the fence-sitter, in most cases, doesn't really sit. It only seems that way to disparaging partisans on either side. What she really does is hop wildly from side to side, depending on the particular issue being attacked or advanced. Besides getting winded, a woman who adopts this life-style can end up with deep frown-lines, identity crisis, and terminal paranoia.

The greatest danger, however, is neither anxiety nor paranoia, nor even indecision. It's the risk you run of being branded traitor by *both* sides.

Pardon me for being personal, but take my case. (And surely there's a pro bono lawyer somewhere who will!) After I went to Mexico City in 1975 for the International Women's Year (IWY) Tribune, along with thirty-five other Utah women, I wrote a simple, straight-forward feature article about the trip for the *Salt Lake Tribune*. I quoted some of the tour members on their impressions, gave one or two innocuous personal reactions, and had a lot to say about the pyramids and the colorful turbans of the African delegates. (Admittedly a pretty blah account, but then I wasn't much of a feminist in 1975. On the other hand, there are those who say I'm not much of a feminist now, which is my point exactly!)

The day after the article appeared, one friend of long standing called another friend of even longer standing to report that the women in her neighborhood were sounding the alarm. They feared my church membership might be in jeopardy because I had written about the conference. (Bear in mind that this was *two years* before the *Utah* IWY skirmish.) The next time I went to dinner at a friend's home, I felt like Angela Davis at a Kennecott Stockholders' meeting. Fire one from the right!

The following fall I went to a conference of the Women Historians of the Midwest in Minnesota. Two other Utahns went also, one a Latter-day Saint woman I knew quite well, who thought, spoke and dressed pretty much as I did. (The term she herself used for the dress style was "Mormon Dowdy.") The other Utahn was a lean University of Utah faculty member who wore levis, braids, and occasionally just jogging shorts and a T-shirt.

Two days into the conference, the jogger was taken aside by her Eastern feminist friends and asked what in the world she could possibly find to talk about with those two Mormon women she'd been seen with. This time I felt like Carrie Nation in a singles' bar and an axeless Carrie at that. Fire one from the left!

At least I'm not alone in experiencing this kind of schizophrenic jolt. Two Salt Lake City women who are in the very forefront of the feminist movement in the state (and thus considered foaming radicals by a good share of the local citizenry) went to a women's conference in San Francisco, where they were openly sneered at in a meeting as "overdressed, elitist grandmothers."

Or take Houston. I went to the National IWY Conference in

Houston with a high heart and a predisposition in favor of most of the propositions—claiming just a couple of exemptions. I hadn't been off the plane five minutes—still standing inside the railings waiting for my baggage to swirl off the conveyor belt—when a woman in bib overalls and lineman's boots came up to tell us about a "Know Yourself" anatomy workshop and self-help clinic that some women were hosting that afternoon in a downtown hotel suite. I gathered that it was a B.Y.O.S. affair—Bring Your Own Speculum. Devout coward that I am, I was so unnerved I was ready to take the next Greyhound back to Utah, stitching in a protective drawstring around the bottom of my long skirt as I went.

But of course I stayed in Houston. And when I attended (because I had an assignment to do so) the "Pro-Family" rally being held across town in the Astrodome as part of the Thumb-Your-Nose-at-IWY campaign, I stepped out of the taxi to see a huge sign lettered (please forgive me, but this was my dose of "welcome-to-reality" medicine): "We Don't Need Kikes and Dykes." Another read: "Five Million Dollars from the J-E-W-S spells I.W.Y." I was sick to my stomach and sick at heart. The two hours spent inside the building didn't improve my spirits. Constantly in my line of vision was a sign four feet by four feet which read, "RIGHTEOUSNESS EXALTETH MISSISSIPPI." I went out looking for a place to buy some bib overalls or a speculum—or both.

Even my women's book club seems confused about which side it's on. I joined the club in hopes of building a good feminist library—and I thoroughly enjoyed my first year, reading great books by Elizabeth Janeway, Doris Lessing, and Marilyn French. Then one day I got a book I hadn't meant to order. (You know the kind of deadline arrangements the book clubs have: if you don't return the little postcard in time, you get the entire contents of the now-defunct West Boot, Montana, Public Library in the next mail.)

But I flipped casually through this unordered book, keeping an open mind. After all, if this was something the other club members felt strongly about, who was I to demur? Suddenly, amid some breath-takingly explicit photographs, I read an account of a campfire session the author had presided over in company with an encounter group she had formed. Only instead of telling ghost stories or singing "Tell Me Why," this group was, and I quote, "invoking the spirit of Mother Orgasm."

I slammed the book shut and ran down the street after the mail carrier's jeep, heaving the book in its back window as it rounded the turn.

Lately, however, the book club has been sending me sheaves of propaganda for such items as "Eighteen Things You Can Make Out of Shell Macaroni Besides Food" and "Macrame Your Way Through the Menopause." Their identity crisis must be even bigger than mine — but then, they're younger.

Let me return to the Houston experience for one last example. When we flew home, virtually all the Utahns, whether pro, con, or supposedly neutral press, came in the same plane. The anti- group took over the front of the cabin (non-smoking area, you see), the pro- the rear half. Appropriately enough, I sat in the middle of the plane.

Before long, a woman in the front got up and began passing a box of chocolates around among her sister delegates. When she came to the midway point, she paused, smiled graciously, and offered me a chocolate. (I abstained.) Then she went back to her seat.

When she had left, a woman across the aisle, by her own definition a militant feminist, asked me, "Why did she offer you a chocolate but none of us?"

I thought about the question a moment. Then I looked her in the eye and said, "I'm a double agent."

I feel that way a lot.

But in my best moments, I know the feeling is misguided. It may seem as if Utah women are divided into two armed camps, with battle lines not only drawn but set in our famous granite. It may appear that the No-Woman's-Land in the middle is vast and unpopulated. But I don't believe it.

From feminists themselves among the most radical, I have time and again heard an urgency about values such as growth, family stability, the needs of children, and how the institution of marriage can best be nurtured — all values that "non-feminists" claim as their priorities. From women who loudly assert that they are not for "women's liberation," I have repeatedly heard fervent opposition to inequity on the basis of sex, rigidity of roles, and people living other people's lives for them — all values that are dear to feminists.

I am not saying anything so simplistic as "We all want the same things." By and large, I believe we do all want many of the same things. But as long as women have the wisdom to distinguish between the means and the end, and to insist that the end does not justify the means, we will have arguments about the means, about how to achieve those goals we share.

But do we have to have double agents? Obviously, no person of integrity can talk out of both sides of her mouth, supporting one stand on an issue at one moment and another later, according to expediency. But must we buy our issues by the gross, in a Saran-wrapped "please-do-not-remove-individual-popsicles" package? Is it possible for women who have alliances and allegiances in both camps to feel doubly supportive instead of doubly disloyal?

I don't know the answers to those questions. I can say that I agree with Emerson: "A foolish consistency is the hobgoblin of little minds." And surely it's clear from what I've said so far that I find myself, at different times, on the left, the right, and in the middle. But I may not be a good example of fence-jumping: frequently I lack the courage, nerves, and judgment to clear the hurdles with grace. But I intend to keep jumping.

In the meantime, I think I'll go see what the book club has sent me this month.

THREE

High on Huckleberry Hill

Nostalgia food. I've been thinking about it quite a bit lately. Nostalgia food engenders rich and cherished memories, so that the food takes on an aura quite separate from its objective reality.

I first learned about nostalgia food when I traveled to Wales, home of my father's ancestors, and tasted the "Poor Man's Cake" that my father had raved about for years. Well, "Poor Man's Cake" is just what its honest title suggests — a make-do dish that barely qualifies as dessert at all. Why, then, had my father carried on about it throughout my childhood? Simply because it was a staple of his childhood, of those times when a growing boy's appetite provided the tangy sauce for any dish, and because his adoring mother made it for him. His memories had virtually nothing to do with the austere ingredients of the humble cake itself.

Nostalgia food from the Intermountain region, according to people who have 'fessed up to me, includes lettuce and milk (lettuce crumbled in a bowl, sprinkled with sugar and doused in milk), cake and milk (same scenario — with canned fruit added if available), and of course the honored Mormon tradition, bread and milk. As for my own family, I was in college before I realized that many people never ate lettuce sandwiches—just lettuce and mayonnaise on bread. We also poured ketchup in a saucer and dipped bread into it. We did the same, I regret to say, with syrup and bread.

But the real nostalgia food of my childhood was huckleberries. Huckleberries and blueberries are first cousins—same family but different genus. One of the earliest memories of my life centers on cool summer mornings in northern Pennsylvania, before the sun had warmed the day, when a swarthy woman known only as "Huckleberry Mary" came sauntering through the alleys of our childhood calling that wonderful chant, "Huu-ckle-berries!" On her head she balanced a large dishpan filled with berries she and her children had picked before sunrise that day. My grandmother would give me a peck measure, and I would scoot out and get our morning's supply. The deep-purple berries were rinsed in cold water, covered with sugar and milk (not today's 1-percent or even 2-percent), and slowly, almost meditatively, consumed. You could put them on cereal, of course, or in muffins or pancakes, but to me, such arrangements always obscured the point, which was the plump, perfect berries themselves. No fruit I know of is plumper than a ripe huckleberry—you might almost call it over-inflated. To feel the berries burst on your tongue and yield up their sweetness— that was a pleasure that never lost its delight.

Now, in actuality, huckleberries have a rather . . . what can I say that will be honest yet not disloyal? . . . a simple flavor. I know that objectively, strawberries and peaches and other fruits are more impressive. But beauty is in the taste-buds of the beholder, so to speak. The other day at Albertson's I saw cups of blueberries for sale. Not quite huckleberries, but family is family. I took them home, washed them lovingly, and poured on some half-and-half. I expected a degree of disappointment. But no. Suddenly, I was five years old again, and the morning was cool, the world fresh, and Huckleberry Mary's street-chant was strong and alluring as ever, unmuffled by time's long corridor.

FOUR

The Meeting

S*cene*: Inside a large, conventional meeting house. There is the usual pre-meeting hubbub. Women are busily conferring with one another over agenda and announcements; at the door, two women are shaking hands with members of the congregation as they enter, trying diligently to call each entrant by her name.

The men are hurriedly urging children into pews, settling quarrels and trying to arrange seating so that the least mayhem will ensue. Some of the men do a better job than others at juggling their paraphernalia: in addition to diaper bags and bottles of apple juice or milk, most have "quiet books," small toys, and some have rather large and cumbersome Primary materials to hang onto and keep track of.

Three or four younger men are radiantly absorbed in small bundles wrapped in fancy crocheted afghans; their fuzzy-headed infants are all dressed in special finery for the occasion, and the seats immediately around them are filled with smiling, wet-eyed grandfathers, uncles, brothers; and over the heads of the crowds, we can see visiting teachers nodding their assurance that they will be ready when the moment presents itself.

Presently, a confident, comfortable-looking woman in her late forties takes her seat on the stand. She is almost immediately flanked by two others: a slender, dark-suited woman of about thirty who keeps whispering last-minute information to the woman in the center; and a woman of perhaps sixty who appears totally unflappable, as if, having engineered reconstruction after the Flood and supervised logistics during the Exodus, she is scarcely about to be intimidated by anything the present moment might demand of her.

Behind them, on the second row, sit four men of varying ages, each in black trousers, white shirt, and black tie.

The youngest of the three women, whose name is Abbot, steps to the pulpit. She smiles silently at the buzzing congregation for a few moments, and as the crowd quiets, we hear a tiny voice call out boldly, "That's MOMMY!" Abbot smiles benignly at the child, while the father, seated in the second pew, blushes, puts a hand gently over the child's mouth, and shakes his head hopelessly at his neighbor.

ABBOT: Sisters and brothers, it's time to begin. We welcome you all here, members and visitors and friends, and hope your time with us will be pleasant. Now I'm afraid we have a large number of announcements today, but they are all important, so we ask for your attention.

To begin with, Brother Hales of the elders group has asked me to tell you that our lovely brethren are collecting empty one-quart oil cans, to be used by the group in making special Christmas projects. They are going to construct Christmas tree stands, candle molds and toys from these used oil cans, I'm told. Elder Hales has placed a large carton outside the south entrance and would appreciate it if you'd all deposit your empty oil cans there, and in so doing contribute to this worthwhile project.

Next, we want to remind you of the Education Week program early next month. Four of our members will be participating, and I'm sure we'll all want to attend and take advantage of this special opportunity. Sister Lorraine Larson will be giving a lecture on "Eschatology and Ether in the Perspective of the Book of Revelation." Sister Ellen Hemming is speaking on "The Gnostic Scrolls and Our Concept of Spirit Translation." Brother LeRuth Davis will have a workshop titled "Twenty Tips for Keeping a Tidy Garage," and Brother Terry Joe Jones will repeat last year's popular series on "Being a More Masculine You."

12

Brother Allen informs me that the quorum is having a special fireside this next Sunday evening with two important guest speakers. Sister Amanda Ridgely Knight will discuss "The Role of Man: Where Does He Fit in the Eternal Plan?" And Sister Alice Young Taylor will lecture on "Three Important Men from Church History."

Next weekend is a big one for the younger teens in our congregation: the Beehive class is going to kayak down the Green River, under the direction of Sister Lynn Harrison. And as I understand it, the deacons will be here at home, helping to fold and stamp the ward newsletter.

In the Young Men's meeting tonight, the boys will have something special to look forward to—a panel of Laurels from the stake will discuss "What We Look for in Boys We Date." Here's your big chance boys!

Now finally clipped to your programs you see a proposal—and I stress that that is all it is so far—for a method of handling our financial commitments for this next year. This is of vital importance to *every member*. I stress that. We want *every one of you* to go home, gather your husbands and children around you, examine this proposal, and decide if you can give us your sustaining vote on it.

(At this point, the third woman on the stand, whose name is Chaplin, gets up and whispers briefly to the speaker.)

ABBOT: Sister Chaplin reminds me that the basketball team will be practicing this week in preparation for the stake play-offs Saturday. Practice will be every afternoon this week from 4 until 6. Coach Tanner has asked that every player get there right at four, or a little before, if she can. Young women, we want you to know how proud we are of you! In the same vein, the *boys'* basketball team has also been doing nicely; if I'm not mistaken, they are leading the region and also have a game sometime this next month. Practice for the boys' team will be over in the old stake house from 5 to 6:30 a.m. this next week. Any boy having a basketball is asked to bring it, since we're a little short on equipment for the boys' team.

Well, I think that's all of the announcements. We will open the meeting by singing on page 102, after which Brother Donny Dee Williams will give the invocation.

The chorister steps to his stand and leads the congregation in the following song:

We are cooking, daily cooking
Food that strengthens, food that fills,
Casseroles that feed the starving,
Wheat from ever-turning mills.

Wheat that's grown and ground and garnished,
Wheat that's fiber-rich and pure,
Wheat for woman, to sustain her,
As she labors strong and sure.

After the prayer, Abbot returns to the pulpit.

ABBOT: I am happy to report that our numbers are growing: we have had six babies born this last month alone! I'll just mention each one, and you can congratulate the happy parents after service.

Sister Jean Hammond and her husband Dale have a new little girl, to be named Rachel Sariah Hammond. Sister and Brother Ellen Taylor, a girl to be named Ellen Fielding Taylor, Jr. Sister and Brother Margaret Jones, a girl to be named Elizabeth Eleanor Jones. As you know, this baby is Sister and Brother Jones' sixth, but the very first girl they've managed to have, and I just want to share with you what Margaret said this past week. Someone who didn't know the family asked her how many children she had. "Six," she said, "and they're all girls but five!"

Now in case you think we've forgotten the opposite sex, Sister and Brother Anne Henderson are welcoming a little boy to their home; he's to be named LeWinky Henderson. Gale and Jimmy Jenson also have a new boy, to be named Tippy Tom Jenson; and Meredith and Billy Joe Gordon have a son whom they have named Fortitude Oak Gordon.

Well, our congratulations to all the families and their new members.

Right now, it's time for a special number from our Singing Fathers. They will announce their own selection.

(The four men dressed in black trousers come to the front of the stand, cluster together, place their arms on each other's shoulders, and set themselves for singing. At this point, one man whispers to another, who steps forward.)

QUARTET MEMBER: We will sing "O My Mother."

O my Mother, Thou that dwellest in the high and glorious place,

When shall I regain Thy presence, and again behold Thy face?
In Thy holy habitation, did my spirit once reside?
In my first primeval childhood, was I nurtured near Thy side?
For a wise and glorious purpose Thou has placed me here on Earth,
And withheld the recollection of my former friends and birth,
Yet ofttimes a secret something whispered, "You're a stranger here,"
And I felt that I had wandered from a more exalted sphere.
I had learned to call Thee Mother, through Thy Spirit from on high,
But until the key of knowledge was restored, I knew not why.
In the heavens are parents single? No, the thought makes reason stare.
Truth is reason. Truth eternal tells me I've two parents there.
When I leave this frail existence, when I lay this mortal by,
Mother, Father, may I meet You in Your royal courts on high?
Then, at length, when I've completed all You sent me forth to do,
With Your mutual approbation let me come and dwell with You.

After the song, Abbot returns to the pulpit.

ABBOT: Thank you very much, brothers, for that special number. Now our speaker today, sisters and brothers, is a returned missionary from our congregation, Sister Eve Wentworth. Sister Wentworth filled a highly successful mission to Japan, was made a district supervisor after she had been out only twelve months, and in due time became Second Counselor to President Mariko Yashimoto of the Nagoya Japan Mission. I happened to meet President and Brother Yashimoto at conference last month, and she told me there wasn't a missionary in their mission who had been a finer example of dedication and leadership than Sister Wentworth. We're happy today to hear from Sister Eve F. Wentworth.

(In the interests of saving space and avoiding repetition, we here give, instead of Sister Wentworth's complete speech, a copy of the ward clerk's notes thereon.)

SPEAKER: Sister Eve F. Wentworth, recently returned missionary.

Summary of remarks: Missionary work—the central calling of House of Israel. Reason Israel was chosen of God. Greatest thing we can do to bless world in anguish. All worthy women to shoulder this responsibility. Mission also the making of character. Boys must help young women prepare for calling. Must never tempt young women or cause them to fall. Tight pants, dangers of. Bare chests an abomination before Lord. Boys don't understand female nature, how easily ignited. Must set example. Not to be cause for some young woman's unworthiness to serve mission. Use time when women are on missions to improve selves, prepare for marriage, prepare to be companion to returned missionary, conduit whereby spirits of women are sent to earth. Can be learning skills—gardening, yard work, home repair, etc. Young women to be serious about missions—cosmic in scope. Eternal consequences. Work affects ages yet unborn, fate of nations. Prepare well. Study scriptures in depth; learn languages; social skills. Avoid getting serious abt. boys prior to call. Boys—charming distractions. Then recounted her own experiences from mission—healing sick, rebuking spirits, receiving revelation abt. impending catastrophe, directing district missionaries out of danger. Value of gentlemen missionaries. Did much good, worked right along with sisters. Need more of right kind of brother missionaries in field. Closed with testimony of work.

Closing song: "Come All Ye Daughters of God."
Closing prayer: Sister Hannah Ruth Williams

FIVE

Matriotism

Last month was February. (Actually, it seems as if the last three months were February, but you can take that up with the weatherman.) February always ranked as the most patriotic month of the year during my childhood. In school, we seemed to spend forever cutting out silhouettes of Lincoln and smearing brown Crayolas over our wobbly drawings of log cabins; no sooner had the library paste dried than it was time for cherry trees, hatchets, and pictures of George Washington with his funny pony tail and grim smile. July couldn't touch February for patriotism, mainly because we weren't in school and thus didn't get so worked up with arts, crafts, and classroom pageantry. And of course, July never got the double dose of attention where I hail from that it receives in Mormon country.

Be all that as it may, I got thinking last month about whether I am really patriotic. And that's when I decided we need a new word; so I coined one.

Matriotic.

Now think about it. "Patriotic," of course, comes from the Latin *pater*, meaning father; a patriot is one "who loves and loyally or zealously supports his own country" or fatherland. A perfectly good word for a perfectly good feeling. "Matriotic," by analogy, comes from the Latin *mater*; a matriot is then one who loves and loyally or zealously supports her motherland, her own planet—Mother Earth.

The two words are not perfectly analogous, fortunately, otherwise people might see conflict of interest where there is none. Patriotism, as we use the word, is about the flag, and the government, and the history of a nation; in our case, the Bill of Rights, free elections, and the peaceful transfer of power, even after a national trauma like Watergate or the Iran-Contra Affair.

Matriotism, on the other hand, is yin to patriotism's yang. It's about the Earth, not the world. It's about what those fortunate few have seen from spaceship portals, not what we see on a map or a globe with regularly updated borderlines and political color-coding. Matriotism is about one sun by day and one moon by night, a moon that waxes and wanes and marks months and menses whether you live in Moscow, Idaho, or the other Moscow. It's about what human beings have felt since the dawn of time when they lay on their backs on the ground and looked up at floating clouds or glittering stars.

Patriotism has always had a lot of the zest of competition in it—rival teams, us and them, Britain's battles being won on the playing fields of Eton, and all that. My country, right or wrong. My country over the other countries.

Matriotism, by contrast, recognizes that while there may be six- or seven-score fatherlands, there is only one mother-land. There are political divisions that have risen, prospered, and utterly vanished, civilizations and great cities that are no more. But while we have her, there is only one Mother Earth. She's done a little rearranging from time to time, what with volcanoes and earthquakes and such. But last spring I stood on a grassy meadow in England and was informed that the same trees I was seeing, the same boulders, the same stream, had been seen and touched by Anglo-Saxons, by Romans, by Stone Age Brits. Many cultures, patriots of many nations—but one earth. Some call her the Spaceship Earth today.

So it's not either-or; it's not a matter of patriotism vs. matriotism. It's just a matter of bringing our matriotism a little more to the forefront perhaps.

For instance, we could start with a holiday. A matriotic holiday, a worldwide day of celebration, gratitude, and rededication to the planet. We'd need a flag, of course; there is that Olympic flag with the colored rings, but frankly I can't get very stirred up about what looks a lot like beer rings on a table surface. But that would do for starters, until we got something better. And we'd need a song—an anthem, really. Wouldn't it be quite a feeling to have an international anthem (no, not the *Internationale*) that little kids all over the world would learn to sing about the oceans and the mountains and the sands and the snows of Earth? We could certainly work up a pledge of allegiance: "I pledge allegiance to the soil, and to the air we breathe, to every species beneath the sun . . . " Well, you get the idea.

We'd certainly need a Matriots' Hall of Fame someplace—maybe onboard a ship that would sail from country to country, celebrating the great matriots who fought for Mother Earth, whether by saving the whales and the gorillas and the snail darters, or by engineering new strains of seed that would feed more on less, or by finding the key to practical mass use of solar energy instead of fossil fuels—and so on.

Some people might not get too excited about being matriotic, seeing that it lacks that old competitive edge. On the other hand, remember what Pogo said: "We have met the enemy, and they is us." This fight to save Mother Earth could end up the biggest battle of all.

And besides: just think what first- and second-graders could do in the way of decorations!

SIX

Testing, Testing . . .

Recently I spent part of a day in the hospital for minor surgery. Actually, even the word "minor" is a bit exaggerated for what I had done. I am now convinced that the doctor could have taken care of everything quite nicely in his office waiting room, or maybe in the front seat of my car, with the engine idling. Nevertheless, it was an experience.

First of all, to make sure it wasn't too much of an experience, I extracted a promise from the doctor—that I would not be subjected to afterburn. "Afterburn" is the principle whereby you spend four hours, for example, cleaning up the mess your kids made preparing a Mother's Day breakfast which you ate in seven minutes. Afterburn is what can make a week-end vacation a week-long misery, if you have mountains of laundry, two cases of second-degree sunburn, one case of poison ivy, one cold and four over-extended credit cards to cope with after the vacation.

Well, bearing that in mind, I made the M.D. swear there wouldn't be any ritual shaving in preparation for my little encounter with the knife. I wasn't about to undergo a fifteen-minute operation followed by six weeks of rash, itching, and general petits miseres which have nothing "petit" about them. "After all," I told the doctor, "if you were going to remove a man's tonsils, you wouldn't shave his moustache, would you?" We negotiated, and he agreed. I thought I was safe, but I was wrong. I had forgotten the tests.

After the initial arrangements are made, patients don't get to just go home and gnaw their nails until the big day. No siree! They have to have Tests. Modern American medicine is founded on Tests. It's the medical profession's way of carrying on the tradition of multiple choice from school days, only now they play the game by giving tests, instead of taking them. But the object seems about the same.

And if you haven't played Tests recently, you're in for a surprise. Between them, the M.D.'s and the technologists (hereafter known as They) have come up with tests that are rare feats of the imagination. For example, they have one test whereby they can take a picture of your innards without using X-ray or fluoroscope. I think it's done with sound waves, and they use it frequently to check the condition of the unborn child in pregnant women. One problem with this gadget is that sometimes the patient's bladder gets in the way of what they really want to see. So to get the bladder up and out of the line of fire, they force you to drink several drums of water. Now you may think you ordinarily drink a lot. But whatever you customarily drink is just a piddling amount compared with what these technicians are determined to get down you.

Then, when they have filled you up to the proper level, they strip you naked, toss you a wisp of a gown as a nod in modesty's direction, and shuffle you out into a public corridor to wait. There you are, five or ten of you, with bare bums held by the force of suction in uncomfortable scoop-bottomed chairs, all pretending to be engrossed in "The Days of Our Lives," which is blaring forth from its perch near the ceiling. Meanwhile, the days of your own life are going by all too slowly, and you soon have the feeling that your very lungs are afloat. In half an hour or so, you are called into the dark sanctorum to have your abdomen scanned with a little implement attached to a huge machine that looks more like a metal detector than a medical instrument.

Slowly, s-l-o-w-l-y, the two women operating the machine sound your depths, taking their time, with occasional breaks to consult each other about what the cafeteria may be offering for lunch that day. When at last you are finished, you're still not finished. Relief is not yet at hand. The technicians have to take the computer printout to the radiologist, to see if all went well, or whether Take Two is necessary. So you sit some more, your legs crossed in at least three places. At last, tests verified, you are ushered to a little restroom that by this time has assumed the aura of Valhalla.

There's another test you'll want to check into some day. This one takes about twelve hours, all told. It begins the night before, when you stop eating or drinking. "No gum, no Lifesavers, no diet drinks, nothing," their advance woman spells out on the phone. You ask if it's okay to swallow.

Next morning at 8:00, at the lab, they want to draw your blood. Now, my family physician used to have a nurse called Gondola, or Granola, or some exotic name. Whatever her name, she could zero in on a vein in my arm, shoot the needle in, draw blood, and be back at the desk yelling at the insurance company on the phone in one revolution of the second hand on the old wall clock. I mean it. Since her retirement, subsequent nurses have acted as if I were deliberately hiding my veins on them. I will spare you what I have gone through trying to give them a small sample of blood. I swear I'm going to have the place tattooed, with a caption reading, "Siphon here."

Anyway, at 8:00 a.m., a tall skinny boy plays hide-and-seek for a while, finds the vein, and draws blood. Then he gives me something to drink, three ounces of a liquid that causes my toes to clench. He gives me another 3-ounce cup and asks for a urine sample. I will also spare you the instructions printed on a sign in the bathroom telling you how to get the sample. All I can say is that it does not seem like an operation for a person with only two hands.

Emerging moderately successful, I place the tiny, damp cup on a counter, where unseen hands later whisk it away for analysis. That's all there is to this test, except that these steps are repeated four times—every hour on the hour. I sleep in the car in the parking lot some of the time, read some of the time. Each time I re-enter the hospital lab, a different young person is there to bleed me. Perhaps it is also a test for them. Perhaps they are drawing straws behind the counter. Who knows? Maybe it's their way of relieving the monotony for me. By noon I have spent longer at this than I will spend in the hospital on the day of the operation.

On that day, incidentally, I am told to bring a "specimen." That's the euphemism so universally accepted that you are never told a specimen of what. Now a great many women bringing in specimens seem to have a pantry full of empty baby-food jars, just the right size. Not me. I searched and searched for something, but all I could find was a quart canning jar. (That is, if you discount some smaller vases; somehow, I really didn't think they'd appreciate my depositing a bud vase on their counter.) When I gave the nurse the bottle as I checked in, she looked at it, about 4/5 full, and said drily, "We only need a small specimen. Just what did you think we were going to do with it, anyway?"

Before very long, I am wheeled in a bed to a holding area. This is it! The real thing! Doctors, nurses, orderlies, aides—they are all coming and going. I strain my ears. I keep my eyes alert. After all, I'm no green kid. I know what goes on in places like this. I watch "General Hospital" and "St. Elsewhere" and "Trapper John" reruns and all the rest. Why, I can go back a lot farther than that—I remember "Joyce Jordan, M.D." and "Young Dr. Malone" on radio. I know the passion that seethes beneath those crisp white uniforms. I know of the triangles, the trysts, the temptations.

That is when the great revelation comes. I listen and I eavesdrop. And do you know what? It's not "General Hospital." It's Safeway. So help me. Everybody is talking about when they are going to take their break, and who will take the afternoon shift for whom three weeks from yesterday. I'm in the holding tank or whatever for about an hour, before and after, and that is all I hear, word of honor. Of course, the doctor is not talking about his break. He is talking about his vacation, which apparently begins as soon as I come out of the anesthetic and can tell him how many thumbs he has on his right hand.

I am home by one o'clock, just in time to see if they've discovered a cure for Diana's amnesia, and if Brad has found out that his baby is not really dead. I notice that they are sending Joe in for some tests. Well, that takes care of him until Christmas!

SEVEN

Passage into Pantyhose

Odd, isn't it, how our memories occasionally go blank on some of life's key moments? Search as I might, I can't remember a thing about the first time I put on a pair of pantyhose.

(Other things we never forget. Rayna Green, one of the country's foremost folklorists, claims that every woman over fourteen has a "first Tampax" story to tell, with details seared into the brain cells. It's the female equivalent of our combined generation's question: "Where were you when you heard of JFK's death?")

But back to pantyhose. I got thinking about that when I was mulling over the ways our lives change behind our backs, so to speak. Whole cultural patterns fade, and we aren't even aware of it. Somewhere during the past couple of decades, American womanhood made the shift from hosiery per se to pantyhose, and an entire way of life veered off in a new direction. But try as I might, I can't remember when it happened to me. Knowing myself, I can conclude pretty definitely that it was some time after the rest of the country had made the switch, but that doesn't help much.

24

The thing is, there is such a cultural and connotative difference between hosiery—stockings—and pantyhose. "Silk stockings"—the very phrase has glamour! Why, they even made a movie with that title. And they used to say that a G.I. on leave in Europe during W.W. II could have a great time for himself with just a pair of nylons and a pack of cigarettes. In fact, if he were in Paris, he could get along without the cigarettes. And, I remember that in Trenton, New Jersey, during the early Forties, if a store was lucky enough to get a shipment of nylons in, the mobs would match the New Year's Eve Times Square crowd for size. I was a child then, not even a teenager, and one of my chores was standing in line with ration books and red and blue points to buy meat and sugar and other scarce goods. I was not yet one of those who would storm the local emporium in hopes of winning the prize of a pair of 15-gauge, 50-denier, but I knew they were mighty important, and I assumed that when I was a woman, the nylon-lust would rise within me, and I would go forth, ready to kill for my two lengths of gauze.

A silk stocking, as I was saying, was frequently a cherished souvenir for men, a memento, the male's version of a corsage crushed in the scrapbook. Can you imagine a man today treasuring a pair of *pantyhose*?

Putting on your first pair of hose (and heels; the words went together, "hose and heels." Dress for a dance was specified as "hosenheels.")—putting on your first pair constituted a rite of passage, an initiation act at least as significant as a boy's first shave. I can remember with great vividness sitting in my friend Carol's living room while she held the top of her outflung first stocking, extending her leg and preparing to draw the stocking on as she would a hip boot. If you got the hose on successfully, without starting the dreaded run, you then launched into the session with the heels, an experience similar in many ways to learning to ride a bike, except we had no training wheels, although we surely could have used them.

(This whole transformation had its sad side, to which I am even now not fully reconciled. To take a free-running young girl who has known the joy of the earth under her feet and who has operated her body with speed, dexterity and confidence, and to shackle her so that she can only teeter and totter and mince and clop woodenly—how far removed is that from foot-binding?)

If the feet were the only things involved, it wouldn't have been so bad. But I remember the day when my mother decided I was to wear a suit to school, complete with girdle. In the first place, I went to the "country mouse" high school, not the city school. My classmates and I were definitely lower-middle class. The tailored, forest-green suit that my mother sent me off in that day was as exotic in that time and place as a muu-muu would have been. Of course everyone asked me why I was "so dressed up." I think I invented a story about having an interview after school. I wasn't as good at the social lie then.

Far worse than the questions was the girdle. Now, I don't know how it happened, but I must have worn that suit and girdle with bobby sox and saddle shoes, because I know for a fact that nothing anchored the girdle (not a panty girdle). I did not, in other words, have nylons hooked to the girdle. By noon, the girdle had rolled itself neatly up on my body and was clamped tightly around my mid-section like a life-preserver. I was suffocating, physically, emotionally, psychologically. It felt as if I were playing host to a powerful and affectionate python.

That must have been around 1952. The next twenty years are a blank, as far as hose go. We come now to 1975. Planning a trip to Europe, I carefully pack everything I need, except a girdle. This lack comes home to me when I put on a hose and find I have nothing to anchor them to. I visit a number of stores in Paris to buy elastic, and make myself some garters, which don't do the job. I have a choice between wearing two tourniquets, which will keep my hose up and bring about acute gangrene, or two loose garters, which permit the hose to slither slowly but inexorably to my ankles while I am presenting the talks for which I have been sent abroad. Apparently, in 1975 I knew nothing about knee-length hose, which would have served fine with the long skirts I was wearing. I told you I was behind the times.

I wish I remembered the details of giving up girdle and hose. All I know is that suddenly my problems involved finding out from the underground where we "full-figured gals," as Jane Russell coyly called us, could get pantyhose that fit. My particular problem is not getting something big enough to go around me. It's that the hose quits and the panty begins before I do, if you see what I mean. The restrictive garment is not conducive to sprinting across Salt Lake City's wide streets before the lights change.

I do have one pair of pantyhose that fits, but it is very, very old, now more in the category of tattered heirloom than part of the current wardrobe. I go everywhere trying to find sisters of the same item, but without luck. I checked out the new Panda Pantyhose. With a name like that, I thought they'd be on the right track. They weren't. People give me pantyhose for birthdays, and various occasions, and I try them on, diligently performing the reverse of the Houdini escape act, without Houdini's success. There are fewer and fewer occasions now for which I wear a dress. I begin to feel the way women must have felt during the Forties. In fact, it comes back to me that most women then used leg make-up instead of the so-scarce stockings—they just slathered liquid make-up on their legs to cover the fish-belly white. But how could I countenance putting make-up on my legs, and not on my face?

By the time I do find pantyhose that fit, color is so unimportant I rarely even consider it, unless it's white. But you know, a favorite hosiery color is "taupe." Honestly, do you know what color "taupe" is? "Brownish gray to dark yellowish brown." No wonder they call it taupe!

As we close in on the magic year 2000, people are giving especially eager attention to what the next century and millennium holds, and whether we are closer to or further away from the Orwellian nightmare vision. I have very little clear picture of what our world will be in fifty or one hundred years, politically, economically, ecologically. But, optimist that I am, I am convinced that if we last that long someone will have devised an improvement on pantyhose. I mean, surely if we can put Sally Ride on the moon, we can give her . . . Well, you get my point.

EIGHT

Reel Goddesses

Film and film images are as important to us today (though not consciously so) as religion was to many of our ancestors in past centuries. They are important because they shape the way we think, hence the way we feel, and thus the way we act. They are as powerfully formative as any religious ceremony.

Molly Haskill, the film critic, writes: "Whatever their roles . . . the women in the movies had a mystical, quasi-religious connection with the public. . . . they were real goddesses."

We in the Nineties may not idolize our film stars as American movie-goers of the Thirties and Forties did, but the power of the silver screen remains mystical. Whatever our backgrounds, I would guess that most of us have spent more hours paying attention to the messages of movies than to sermons and Sunday school lessons in church or synagogue. We may be hazy on our Apostles' Creed, our Articles of Faith, our catechism, but we are razor-sharp on the teachings of Hollywood. Biblical scriptures may be dim in our minds, but who doesn't know the following lines to live by:

"If you want anything, just whistle."

"This is bigger than both of us."

"I don't think we're in Kansas anymore, Toto."

"Come up and see me sometime." (And that even more memorable Mae West line, when an admiring ingenue said, "Goodness, those are wonderful pearls!"—"Goodness had nothing to do with it!")

"Ah, sweet mystery of life!" (Jeanette MacDonald rendition, Madeline Kahn rendition.)

"I had an orgasm once, but my shrink said it was the wrong kind."

"You Jane, me Tarzan."

"If you want monogamy, marry a swan."

My premise here (certainly not original) is that what we see on film affects in a hundred ways our behavior and our concept of ourselves as women and men, whether any of us realize the full influence or not. Thinking from time to time about what Hollywood and TV are preaching can help us make more conscious life choices.

For purpose of analysis, I'd like to use the archetypal concept of the triple goddess as a way of looking at Hollywood's portrayal of women. Traditionally, the myths speak of Woman in three phases: Maiden, Mother, and Crone.

Films have always focused primarily on Maidens—young, beautiful, nubile—from the days when Mary Pickford dressed and performed as America's pinafored Sweetheart (even though she was married and an astute businesswoman at the time) to these days of Brooke Shields and Jodie Foster and Mariel Hemingway and the young women of the Brat Pack—Molly Ringwald, Ally Sheedy, the *Pretty-in-Pink*, *Sixteen Candles* starlets. There is a great deal to be said about Woman as Maiden, about the female role in romance. The essential point here is that the Maiden is young, beautiful, inexperienced (emotionally if not technically a virgin), and she gains her significance in terms of a relationship with a man. She is still Snow White, waiting for her Prince. And she becomes the model for a million daydreams.

Though Woman as Mother has not been a central role in Hollywood movies, it is exactly Woman as Mother who has changed the most in Hollywood's depiction. For decades, Mother meant Anne Revere or Fay Bainter or Spring Byington—sweet-faced, grey-haired, aproned—standing by a window, waiting and worrying. Just as no flesh-and-blood mother can live up to the Mothers Day hype, no real mother, sitting in the darkened theater watching the martyr parade go by, could avoid waves of guilt and self-condemnation. Today in movies, we have vastly more realistic Mothers, more fully human, fully female. Think of all the single mothers we have seen. Remember Sally Field in *Norma Rae*, a tough-talking, hard-working mother of three (each by a different father). Or Sally Field in *Places in the Heart*, the young widow saving the cotton crop. Or Sally Field in *Murphy's Romance*, the young divorcee finding romance with a sixty-year old who admits he's sixty (finally). And that's just Gidget grown up. What about Shirley MacLaine as the mother in *Terms of Endearment*, or Cher's wonderful role in *Mask*?

And what about Woman as Crone? Now wait: don't flinch at the word. Forget wrinkled, raddled, and rejected. In real life, it never has meant any of that, but for many years Hollywood focused on that perception of the mature woman. And we bought the Tinseltown doctrine that Geritol begins at thirty. Today, against great odds, we are shifting the spotlight to other, more realistic roles of that woman in her prime. (Let's all remember and keep quoting Gloria Steinem's great line at her fiftieth birthday party. Whenever anyone said to her, "You don't look fifty," she reminded them, "This is what fifty looks like." Well, maybe all Fifties don't look like Steinem, but we don't all look like Grandma Moses, either.)

Just what is the Crone? Go back to myth and legend. The Crone was a wise woman. One writer says, "The Crone was Wisdom herself . . . anciently dwelling in caves, walking the highways, standing at the crossroads, and making love on the vast seas."

Another historian speaks of Artemis as Crone, whose job was "To assist people who are no longer where they were and not yet where they hope to go." The Crone was also viewed as a seeker, a person in a time of introversion and spiritual search. More than anything else, the Crone was, and is, in the words of writer Vickie Noble, "A woman whole in herself."

This is what the fullness of mythology and history and anthropology says about the Crone. But what has Hollywood shown us? Two kinds of Crones, I think. First, the powerful Crones who are evil, menacing, in short, witches. Judith Anderson made a career out of Crones, highlighted by the controlling, devious,

30

and deadly Mrs. Danvers in *Rebecca*. (She played a similar though smaller role as Memnot in *The Ten Commandments*.) Lining up behind Anderson are a whole host of mean housekeepers, governesses, school-teachers, prison matrons, nurses, and so forth. Again, as Anderson's Mrs. Danvers became mythic in its own right, Louise Fletcher's Big Nurse in *One Flew Over the Cuckoo's Nest* assumed archetypal dimensions. Cloris Leachman parodies these Crones in at least two roles—Nurse Diesel in *High Anxiety* and Frau Blucher in *Young Frankenstein*.

But powerful Crones are too fearsome for Hollywood generally. Film makers have preferred the ineffectual Crone, either sympathetic and powerless—the widow, the aged invalid—or silly and powerless—the sisters in *Arsenic and Old Lace* (reborn as the sisters guarding the Recipe in *The Waltons*), Joyce Grenfell as the daffy school-mistress hopelessly outwitted by the girls of St. Trinian's—you've seen them.

Despite the determination of script-writers and directors *not* to give powerful, positive Crones a central role in film, we in fact have had many memorable Crones. The reasons are several: first, even a small part for a powerful, autonomous woman stands out by comparison with weaker female characters. Mrs. Danvers haunts us; we have to stop and think to remember the nameless narrator (played by Joan Fontaine) in the same film. Whenever Maureen Stapleton shows up in a picture, even for a cameo role, she seems more alive, more *real*, more human than anyone else in the cast. Moreover, many film actresses have projected such strong, self-contained images that almost in spite of the scripts, they have given us mature, positive portraits.

Has Hepburn ever been anything but her own woman, even when cast as the Maiden (as in *Philadelphia Story*)? Hepburn turned every stereotyped "old maid" role into a three-dimensional character of dignity and power. (Think of *Rainmaker, Summertime, The African Queen, The Corn Is Green, Grace Quigley*.)

Think of women who seemed too powerful, somehow out of place, in Maiden roles, only to assume full stature after forty. Joanne Woodward, with a couple of exceptions (*Three Faces of Eve, The Long Hot Summer*), had to wait for her roles, and did one of her greatest turns as the "old maid" in *Rachel, Rachel*. Jane Alexander has come to prominence in her Crone roles—*Eleanor and Franklin, Dear Liar*, etc. Glenda Jackson made her

31

mark on the American audience playing that quintessential Crone, Elizabeth R, and has become stronger and stronger as she leaves the farcical Maiden roles behind to do *Turtle Diary* and similar works. A look at the film *Julia* is revealing—Fonda is the Maiden in that picture and pretty much in the work she's doing even now; Redgrave, by contrast, has always been a Crone figure. (She was miscast, though regally, in *Camelot*. Can we doubt that she should have ended up running, or reforming, the Abbey at film's end?) The list of strong actresses who were almost never given roles to match their power until later in life goes on: Geraldine Page (think of all those neurotic Tenessee Williams roles), Kim Stanley, Julie Harris, Anne Bancroft, Colleen Dewhurst (whom Pauline Kael labels "that giant force of nature"). Was Simone Signoret ever as wonderful as a Maiden as she was as a Crone? (*Room at the Top, Ship of Fools, Madame Rosa, Le Chat*.) European directors seem to know better what to do with mature women, the likes of Melina Mercouri, Irene Papas, Anna Magnanni; it's America that has the obsession with youth.

Maybe, I keep thinking. Maybe when American women refuse any longer to buy into the youth cult, when we don't giggle or lie or hesitate about our ages, when we claim our own power, use it freely and confidently, to heal and to grow, maybe then we will get scripts and movies that do justice to the Crone, especially if, along with all these achievements, we have more women writing, directing, producing. And if we get films glorifying the American Crone (to paraphrase Ziegfeld in a way he would bellow about), then maybe we will celebrate the Crones in our own lives, beginning with ourselves.

I am not, I insist you note, advocating an eclipse of the Maidens' place in the sun. Tragedy, comedy, irony, and romance—each of these, but especially Romance, has a place for the Maiden. But each also has a place for the Crone. All I'm calling for is a little affirmative action in films, a little readjustment of the imbalance. I dream of Things As They Can Be.

A final note to remind us of Things As They Are: Marilyn Monroe, proclaimed by many as the No. 1 Goddess, died more than twenty-five years ago. She is more acclaimed, more written and read about now than ever before. I think that tells us how our culture at the present wants its goddesses—on a pedestal and silent. Dead is no drawback.

NINE

In Memoriam: Algie E. Ballif

The title of this collection, "Only When I Laugh," comes, of course, not from Neil Simon (I had the title before he did) but from the old story about a man who had been run through with a large spear. When asked if it hurt terribly, he replied, "Only when I laugh."

Sometimes it hurts whether we laugh or not.

Recently, Utah lost one of its foremost citizens, Algie Eggertsen Ballif. Her death made many of us hurt. So we're not laughing right now, and if it's all right with everybody, and even if it's not, I'm going to talk about Algie Ballif. If you knew Algie, you'll know why I want to talk about her. If you didn't, I'll try to make clear what you missed.

In an interview I read once, a Southern black woman of limited means and education but unlimited commitment spoke of the breadth of her own civil rights activities over the years: "If it was anything to do with justice, I was there."

Her words apply to Algie Ballif. If there was anything to do with justice, she was there.

I knew her only in the last decade of her long life, as I was drawn into the affairs of the feisty and energetic Alice Louise

Reynolds Forum in Provo. After I had initially made her acquaintance, I began to notice that if there was any meeting of importance going on in Utah County, Algie would be there. I should say "they," because Algie was ever flanked by her lieutenants, her gracious and thoughtful younger sister Thelma, and her friend of sixty-five years, the eloquent, brilliant Helen Stark.

Were the Democrats bravely trying to make their voices heard in Reagan Country? (Utah had the nation's largest percentage vote for Reagan in 1984, and Utah County the largest percentage vote in the state.) Algie and friends were there. Was some expert desperately trying to explain to Happy Valley folk the insanity of nuclear proliferation? Algie was there. Was Justice Sandra Day O'Connor speaking on the campus of Brigham Young University? Algie would be there, you could count on it. Always in my mind's eye I will see the three of them, elegantly dressed in their handsome suits and stylish shoes, their gray hair beautifully coiffed. There they would be on the front row of life, taking notes, asking, with the greatest of tact and diplomacy, the most outrageous questions — the questions which, however hard, had to be asked.

And if the meeting had to do with justice for women, well, in that case, Algie would not only be present, but more than likely she had been one of the moving forces behind the gathering in the first place.

The Alice Louise Reynolds Forum was but one project in a rich lifetime of important work at the national, state, and local levels, but it was the way I came to know Algie and her circle. There isn't time here to tell the story of the organization of the forum, of the efforts and money that went into establishing the Alice Louise Reynolds Room in the Harold B. Lee Library at BYU, and how the women were eventually banished from the room for their controversial activities. We all thought of the forum as our local chapter of the Grey Panthers. They were fighters, never mind that their average age hovered around eighty.

My favorite memory of them as a group spotlights the time they traveled to Salt Lake City to see the satirical musical comedy *Saturday's Voyeur* that, year after year, outrages and offends one segment of the Utah population and delights another. I watched them as, with canes and assistance from younger friends, they struggled up the stairs from the lobby to their seats. The theater staff (men in long ponytails and proud ear-rings, women with orange hair and carefully blasé expressions) looked at each other and rolled their eyes. "They'll be asking for their money back after the first chorus," prophesied one young turk who had not yet learned the truth about appearances. After the first chorus, the forum gang were, in fact, applauding, banging on the floor with their canes, and wiping away laughter-born tears.

They had keen humor, the wisdom of their years, plus connections, know-how, and, most wonderful to some of us in the younger contingent, they had the courage to act.

But then, Algie Ballif had been acting in noble causes all her life. She served two terms in the state legislature. She was named by Eleanor Roosevelt to the education committee of John F. Kennedy's Commission on the Status of Women. She was director of the Utah Division of Public Welfare from 1967-69. She was president of the Provo Board of Education for twenty-three years. She organized and for some years headed the women's physical education department at BYU, where she also taught English and speech.

There's more. A lot more. The citation was long when the Utah Women's Political Caucus presented her with the Susa Young Gates Award, for contributions in the arena of human rights and the cause of women in the state, and when they gave her a Distinguished Woman Award from the University of Utah Women's Resource Center.

Beyond the public person, of course, there was Algie Ballif, wife and mother of four. Her daughter Grethe Peterson remembers hot meals at noon around the dining room table, busy with friends and relatives and lively conversation. Neighbors speak of her wonderful Danish cooking, her magnificent plums that made such fine jam. If, as concerns her church, she was something of a maverick, she was a maverick who nevertheless did not desert the herd, but contributed her talents generously.

All the years I knew her, Algie was legally blind and partially deaf. Dreadful nuisances, of course, but to her mind not worth wasting the time to talk about. Over eighty-five and hard of hearing—and she shamed us all, all who were younger, able-bodied, and less than totally involved. Not that she ever reproached any of us when we flagged, when we grew discouraged, when the travesty of Utah's International Women's Year meeting in 1978 disheartened many. But in our minds, the message was clear: how dare we speak of lost hopes when she, who had been a suffragist fifty years earlier, was not ready to quit?

Many of us at Algie's funeral in 1984 thought about Geraldine Ferraro and wished her selection as the Democratic candidate for vice-president had not so closely coincided with Algie's passing. How Algie would have rejoiced to see that landmark achieved! One speaker at the services said he half expected Algie to send back for an absentee ballot.

Algie—and her equally stalwart sisters, Esther Peterson, for decades a relentless consumer advocate in Washington, D.C., and of course the irreplaceable Thelma, as well as their cousin Virginia Sorensen, renowned writer—all were part of a tradition of *noblesse oblige*. Like the Roosevelts and the Kennedys, the Eggertsens, and in turn, the Ballifs, were brought up to believe that if you had advantages in life—brains, talent, education, means—you owed something to the world, especially to the less fortunate members of the human race. It's a tradition that deserves to be passed on.

At the funeral, speaking with a woman I didn't even know except as someone else who loved Algie, I said, "She was the great role model of my life."

"Ah," the other woman replied. "Then you haven't really lost her."

Only when I laugh.

TEN

Unpacking Interruptus

Many magazines—from *Ladies Home Journal*, which I read as a teen-ager, to *MS*, which I read as a prime-of-lifer, to *Roughing It Raw*, which I read during one dreamy summer when contact with reality was minimal—have published articles about How to Pack. How to pack for a weekend, how to pack for a cruise, how to pack for a ten-day hike into a wilderness so primitive the birds still sport a few scales. But I have yet to read an article about How to Unpack. And that's the one I really need.

I can pack in less time than it takes to settle on a TV channel for the evening. I can pack twice in the time it takes three friends to decide where to have lunch next Tuesday. But I seem constitutionally unable to unpack. Unpacking a small bag used for a sleep-over in Salt Lake City takes me four days. Unloading the week-end bag from a trip to Jackson Hole takes one week minimum. I've now been back ten days from an extended spring trip to Europe, and I don't think I'll see the bottom of the suitcases before Labor Day.

It wouldn't be so bad if it were just a matter of tripping over two fully packed suitcases in the middle of the bedroom. But of course, that's not the situation. The situation is two bags perpetually yawning, trailing their unlovely contents over all available space like the devouring pods from *Invasion of the Body Snatchers*. A pile here, hoping to be laundered. A stack there, waiting to be escorted to the bathroom. A little cluster of presents anticipating delivery as soon as life gets back to normal, ho-ho. The ill-at-ease group of items borrowed for the occasion and not yet returned, silently sending you guilt messages from the dresser. And somehow, the recently returned traveler seems to have a lengthy list of chores and projects far more urgent than unpacking.

Those of you who do not recognize the scenario above are certainly free to leave now if you like. The rest of us will draw our chairs into a circle and convene the Lay Psychologists League for yet another session.

Just what is at the bottom of unpacking interruptus? Is it as simple as the fact that some people are good starters and poor finishers? Does it have to do with afterburn—the complex of mopping-up chores that accompany so many otherwise pleasant activities, from having a spaghetti dinner for eight to tramping with the dogs through the cool, fragrant (burr-infested) woods?

Perhaps it arises from the disparate principles governing packing and unpacking. When packing, we are guided by two concerns: What will I need? and Is there room? Unpacking has a very different and much stickier set of concerns: How come there's not room for this in the closet now if there was before I left? Should I wash this lingerie or just face up to the truth and throw it out? If I keep this combination model-ship-picture-frame-and-candlestick, it will just collect dust, but if I don't keep it as a souvenir of the trip to Cape Cod, will the Codders notice when they come here this fall? Will I really put these theater programs in a scrapbook, or will they simply add to the paper collection mildewing in the basement? This battery-operated so-called mosquito repelling device (bought expressly for the trip) has a money-back guarantee: is it worth my time to write a letter of complaint complete with photographs documenting my mosquito-bite scars, package up the impotent little gadget, tote it to the Post Office, pay for its flight home, etc.—or should I write off its cost as tuition in the Graduate School of U Live and Learn?

Well, let's keep an open mind on the question. Surely there's a paper to be written on the subject—maybe a master's thesis. (I read a thesis once on "How to Wash a Blanket"; the actual title was longer, of course, but that's what it all boiled down to.)

Before we adjourn the meeting, let me throw out one final idea. The real unpacking from a journey doesn't have to do with clothes, toiletries, and accumulated souvenirs. It has to do with experiences, insights, inner changes—what we went away hoping to see and do, what actually happened, what we have brought back with us that we didn't have before, or what we lost along the way. A colleague recently returned from a tour of China and said, "The trip skewed my whole world view. I have a lot of mental re-arranging to do." Whatever happens with the suitcases, we all need to "unpack" in this metaphoric way from journeys that we consider significant. We need to be able to share with those close to us what the experience has meant. If we are lucky, we find people who really care and who want to listen. Some of us use the resources of personal journals to "unpack" in depth. An important truth we women confront is that a great many of us have rarely had opportunities to "unpack" from the ongoing life journey we all take, have had little or no chance to say where we have been and what we have seen and felt. Instead, we have had to keep that precious baggage within ourselves, usually unexamined even by ourselves, all our lives long.

If you wonder why we are seeing more and more published biographies, autobiographies and oral histories of women these days—and not just of so-called distinguished women—the answer is that at last we are starting to value and to search out the still-unpacked treasures from the attics and the basements of women from all neighborhoods of life, past and present.

If you have a trip ahead of you this summer, bon voyage! If you've made yours, welcome home! And as to the unpacking, well, I frequently find inspiration in movie titles. Like *Now, Voyager*. Or *It's Never Too Late*. Or that great classic, *Come September*. Ah yes, that seems to fit.

ELEVEN

When Nice Ain't So Nice

The problem with Nice isn't that it's sometimes wimpy; the problem is that Nice can be dangerous. More crimes have been committed behind the mask of niceness than behind all the ski masks worn to all the convenience store stickups ever perpetrated.

I don't actually intend to talk about literal crimes here, but as long as the subject came up, it's worth mentioning that until the roof caved in, everybody said Utah corporate conman Grant Affleck was a really nice guy. (Nice cuts both ways in giving Utah its title as Fraud Capital of the nation: we produce con men so nice they can't be doubted, and victims so nice they "cain't say no.") Documents forger and bomb killer Mark Hoffman, they said, was nice. Likewise convicted child sex abuser Alan Hadfield—so nice that an entire community rose up to vilify the victims and slander the messenger rather than accept the verdict on their nice-guy neighbor. And, apparently, Ted Bundy was as nice as they come.

I first identified niceness as a culprit with the help of a colleague, Karen Lynn. I told Karen that some of today's college students seem pleasant enough, but somehow unpleasantly resistant at the same time, in a way that was unclear but very real.

"Oh, I know what you mean," Karen said. "The students smile very politely, and the unspoken message goes like this: 'I am a very nice person. I'm sure you are a very nice person too. Therefore I am sure you will give me a nice grade. And if you don't—what's wrong with you?' " Niceness in some students' minds fulfills all obligations that one might otherwise expect to see paid in the coin of effort, intelligence, and results. (Incidentally, John Ciardi spotted the problem in the same setting. He wrote a fine poem called "On Flunking a Nice Boy Out of School." I read it to students from time to time. Some laugh. Some sulk, suggesting tacitly that even reading the poem is not very nice of me.) But I look beyond the classroom to find the arena where niceness is most harmful.

C. S. Lewis praises courage as the virtue that protects all other virtues. That is, it is courage which enables us to be truthful when speaking the truth may be risky; it is courage that backs up loyalty when loyalty is unpopular; it is certainly courage which makes patriotism meaningful in times of danger. By the same logic, I believe it is niceness which can corrupt all the other virtues. Niceness edits the truth, dilutes loyalty, makes a caricature of patriotism. It hobbles Justice, short-circuits Honor, and counterfeits Mercy, Compassion, and Love.

Nice is, among other things, a logic-proof argument (chronically nice students seem puzzled when I try to explain the rationale of penalties for late work; my reasons are all so irrelevant to their niceness), an undiscerning critique (Wayne Booth's mother used to chide him: "Why must you be so critical in your reviews?"), and a silken shackle on the leg of millions of women.

(The list of things nice women don't do includes, but is not limited to, thinking, speaking, moving—in the romantic context—arguing, competing, winning, and laughing out loud. I had a very nice woman tell me once, after I had given some foolish presentation or another to her women's group: "That was hilarious! Really hilarious! I almost laughed out loud!" Heaven forfend!)

Niceness begins in the home; it is taught as a prime doctrine of the "poisonous pedagogy" Alice Miller exposes. Miller, a brilliant Swiss psychologist whose work is assuming major proportions in the field, has traced much neurosis to the philosophy, dominant throughout most of this century, that the role of the child is to be docile, obedient, and subservient to the parent, whose word is law. The "poisonous pedagogy" teaches children, in other words, to be "nice." It demands that children not resist the status quo, not take any direct action against whatever injustices are going down. Thus it indirectly but inevitably encourages covert action, manipulation, passive-aggression, duplicity, and denial. (My mother used to say in so many words: "Be nice. Don't argue with your father. Agree with him, and then slip out the back door and do what you want, like your brothers do." She also said to me with a simper: "Your father is the head of the home, remember that. And I'm the neck that moves the head!" My response to such advice was often a single, very un-nice word.)

As I look around the neighborhood, the campus, the community, and the church, I see one result of these teachings in the way nice people act when they disagree: sentimentally or deviously towards those we encounter face to face, and hostilely towards those we don't know. For thirty years I have been upset and puzzled by the fiercely hostile tone of many Letters to the Editor of BYU's student newspaper. These letters are not merely impassioned, not just full of youthful vigor and sass, not purely angry. They are hostile and mean-spirited. Whether discussing red tape in the Administration Building, parking on campus, or pricing in the Bookstore, the letters drip with innuendo, invective and scripture-laden scourging. All this from neatly dressed, smiling youths who hold doors open for each other and walk clear across campus to turn in stray Number Two pencils to the Lost-and-Found depository.

This same pattern shows up even more dangerously on our highways. The heavy artillery has so far blasted away only on the California freeways, but the nice, friendly, zucchini-sharing people of the Utah culture are not immune to the hostility that spurts out at strangers once we are behind the wheel. Afoot and at home in our own neighborhoods, we silently and smilingly put up with each other's dogs that howl all night long, kids that trample our flower gardens, teens that sun-bathe and wash their cars to ear-shattering heavy metal music. But when we drive out of those neighborhoods, any stranger becomes fair game for our angry honking, cutting in, heading off, not-so-muted swearing, and flipping the bird. I am suggesting that

there is a connection. If niceness did not forbid our direct asser-
tion on dog howls and childish vandalism, perhaps there
wouldn't be quite so much hostility stored up waiting to slosh
out on Interstate-15.

Nice takes other tolls. According to an article in the *Deseret
News*, 11 October 1989, pharmaceutical houses have hard data
showing that Utahns (with a national reputation as your generic
nice people) use huge quantities of tranquilizers and
anti-depressants, far more per capita than the populations of
other states. Depression of course has many causes, but repressed
anger is among the foremost. Anger is punished and prohibited
from childhood in cultures that teach the poisonous pedagogy
and preach the creed of niceness. I fantasize about what life in
Happy Valley might be like if the lid of niceness were eased off
the pressure cooker of emotions.

I worry about hostility on the highways and depression in
the home. I worry about battering and abuse, both physical and
sexual, that seem to be on the rise in places where you wouldn't
expect it. For instance, I learned (without seeking the information) that in my very nice young-executive neighborhood of about
fifteen homes, at least five wives are beaten regularly by their
husbands. One of the nicest men in the ward has been convicted of sexual molestation. Absolutely the nicest elder I knew
in the mission field afterward had to uproot his wife and family
and give up his profession because he had been found guilty of
molesting preschoolers. I seriously wonder: if these men had
been under less pressure to be "nice," would they have been
more in touch with their dark sides—the dark side that we all
have—and thus more able to deal directly with violent impulses
before they became actions?

If the cultural mandate to be Nice has driven men's darker
sides into hiding, what can we say about women, who aren't
even supposed to *have* dark sides? Passive aggression is one of
the milder manifestations of Niceness, seen in the woman who
wouldn't say no to anyone, but who will repeatedly keep you
waiting an hour, or "accidentally" smash the fender on your
borrowed car, or "forget" an important responsibility she promised to manage. More deadly is the Nice Lady who never raises
her voice, never utters the slightest profanity, but whose devas-
tating words and emotional abuse leave permanent scars as dis-
figuring to the soul as any physical battering is to the body.

(Shakespeare's comment on the matter: "Lilies that fester smell far worse than weeds.")

And thus we come to the quick of this terrible ulcer. The creed of niceness does damage to the Self, to the soul. The struggle for personal authenticity is a lifelong one, the true Hero Journey we all must take if life is to have meaning. And the demons with which we grapple in the underworld have many shapes. Some have names long memorialized in literature: Pride, Sloth, Envy, Avarice. Others are more pastel despots: Conformity, Busyness. And Niceness.

How does Niceness threaten the hero on the journey? The Quest is for the authentic Self to discover as many of the particulars as possible from an infinite number of particulars, and especially certain crucial particulars about that totally unique, eternally individual, unceasingly changing Self. And as if this labor were not Herculean enough, the Hero, even as she seeks the True Self, must somehow nurture—that is, foster the growth of—that evasive, elusive Self. Niceness threatens by saying there is no True Self, or that the True Self is synonymous with the Natural Man (and thus an enemy to God), or that the False Self is what we ought to seek.

Permit me a metaphor. Imagine a mother, a Queen, if you like, who awakens from the sleep that follows childbirth to discover that her child has been abducted, carried away. At first there are some signs of the child—a cry down a long corridor, a blanket woven for the baby and discovered on the lawn, perhaps a scent of baby's breath on the night air. These eventually stop. Time passes. The mother searches night and day. And every now and then she hears from the child—a lisping voice over a telephone line, garbled with static; torn parts of a handwritten note; sometimes even a little gift, sent with love. And the mother continues to hunt for her child, to follow clues, and to send the child, by whatever means—on the phone in the fleeting moments permitted, by thought transference, by prayer—all the love and support she can muster, as the search continues.

Now imagine that, in the midst of these labors, the mother is repeatedly beset by concerned people—most prominently the Queen Mother and her consort—who urge her to break off her search, who try to press a different child on her, insisting that this one is much "nicer" than her own, scolding her, saying she is selfish, willful, possibly even crazy to go on with her search. If the opposition is persistent, the Queen may eventually come to believe she *is* crazy, to doubt that there ever was such a child, to cease following the clues, to grow deaf to the voice on the other end of the phone. To give up the search. Devotees of the cult of niceness abandon the True Self and promote the False Self, the self that psychologist John Bradshaw describes this way: "You pretend a lot. You gauge your behavior by how it looks—by the image you believe you're making. You wear a mask, play a rigid role, and hide your emotions. You say you're fine when you feel hurt or sad. You say you're not angry when you are" (*Bradshaw On: The Family* [Deerfield Beach, FL: Health Communications, 1988], 159.) You've heard of the Nicene Creed, the Christian confession of faith first adopted in 325? Now hear the Nice Creed:

> We believe in being Nice,
> in speaking softly at all times, even when loud objection may be more logical;
> in saying nothing in response to minor inconveniences such as being jostled on a bus, or relegated to a back seat, or not being allowed to ride at all, or being run over by the bus;
> and in saying even the most appalling things in soft, non-committal tones, even, if worst comes to the worst, in whispers.
> We guard against silence as against speaking out, for in silence is Thought born;
> therefore, we cultivate and foster small talk, which says naught yet smothers silence.
> We believe that pleasantries are better than truths, friendliness better than honor, jocularity better than Justice.
> We believe that neatness is the end of logic and cleanliness the epitome of order.
> And we most devoutly believe in seeing nothing that is disconcerting or unpleasant.
> We believe in turning the other head, closing the other eye, stopping the other ear, and biting the other tongue.

Etymology often uncovers hidden truths. The word "nice" can be traced back through Middle English to mean strange, lazy, foolish; through Old French to mean stupid or foolish; to the Latin "nescius," meaning ignorant, not knowing. Bear in mind that George Orwell insisted most ignorance is intentional, and you understand the serious danger of niceness: deliberate, lazy not knowing. Not wanting to know, not willing to know, not about to know.

Know what? Why, anything. Anything at all. Not to take one nibble from one piece of fruit of the Tree of Knowledge of Good and Evil, but to remain, instead, Nice. Not to know about History, except for a few pretty branches used as decoration. So much of History is not nice at all. For one thing, those who refuse to ignore history are destined to think about it. Certainly not to know about Poverty. Distinctly not nice. Nice people do not want homeless shelters in their neighborhoods, or their town, if it comes to that; they don't want group homes or halfway houses or soup kitchens; in fact, they are nervous about public benches on the streets unless they are built with dividers to prevent reclining; nice people don't sleep on benches, after all. Not to know about Death, but to confine him to curtained cubicles in isolated "units" of hospitals and nursing homes. Death is unequivocally not nice.

Nice flies under false colors, wants the reputation of the gentle dove without the wisdom of the wise serpent. It is the Great Imposter, having none of the power of Virtue but seeking the influence thereof. Nice is neither kind, nor compassionate, neither good nor full of good cheer, neither hot nor cold. But, being puffed up in its own vanity, it is considerably more dangerous than luke-warmth.

Nice, in short, ain't so nice.

TWELVE

Lay Therapists

Not long ago I wrote about the fact that women have always diagnosed and prescribed for each other's physical ailments. More and more these days we fill yet another role in each other's lives—lay therapist. It's probably a good thing psychiatrists aren't unionized, or many of us would find ourselves at the bottom of the Great Salt Lake wearing cement pantyhose for being non-union scabs.

You may not think of yourself as a therapist; perhaps the most you have ever said is, "I'm a good listener." So? The difference between an amateur listener and a professional one is that the therapist, at the end of fifty minutes, can say, "Your time is up," but the good listener-friend cannot.

Actually from the point of view of the patient, or the client, as she is called these days, a friend has several advantages over a professional shrink:

1. She's cheaper. Even if you carry on your consultations via long distance, it's still cheaper—and the shrink's rates are definitely not lower after 11:00 p.m., in case you've wondered!

2. A friend's terminology is usually much more useful. Jane Howard, in her book *A Different Woman*, explains the simple

code she and her sister have for diagnosing the mental states of
their friends. Here's the breakdown: "Better," "Worse," "The
Same." As in:

"How's Marie?"

"Oh, about the same, What about Lynn?"

"Better, definitely better. And Sandy?"

"Worse, I'm afraid."

Now a shrink would take thirty minutes to convey the same
information, using phrases like "mood swings," "diminished
affect," and "depressive corollary reaction." Who needs it? If
you're in the middle of an emotional crisis, you're hardly interested in playing "Thirty Days to a More Impressive Vocabulary."

In addition to speaking straight from the shoulder, friends
who double as emergency therapists come to know *your* verbal
shorthand. When my friend Anne calls and asks how things
are, if I say, "I'm getting on the bus," I have given her a full
report which she can interpret without any hesitation. She will
know that I am restless, over-burdened, bored, near the end of
my rope, and replaying once again my fantasy of boarding a
Greyhound bus and disembarking 500 miles down the road at
some greasy spoon cafe with a "Dishwasher Wanted" sign in
the fly-specked window. I have never gotten on the bus, of
course, and in fact, as long as Anne is around to be my amateur
analyst, I probably won't need to.

Before leaving the matter of shorthand between friends, let's
take note of the fact that sometimes the shorthand isn't even
verbal. Body language conveys a lot, and most close friends can
speed-read each other's messages. After my last "getting-on-
the-bus" session with Anne, she walked me to my car and bade
me good-bye with a gesture peculiar to us and perfectly precise.
With an upward-spiraling motion of both hands and a nod of
the head with the chin leading, she communicated the following: "All right now; get on with it. Pick yourself up after letting
off all of this steam and don't waste any more time kvetching.
I'm pulling for you."

3. A final advantage of the lay therapist: she doesn't auto-
matically drop off the face of the earth in August. In case you
haven't had to find out the hard way, every paid shrink in the
U.S.A. goes A.W.O.L. in August. If your bio-rhythms sink to
the cellar before Labor Day, tough luck.

Now since we're trying to be honest here and give information grounded in reality, I must admit that friends do have one or two tiny little drawbacks as therapists.

1. First of all, your Good Samaritan shrink hasn't taken the Freudian oath or whatever it is the pros take, so you have to negotiate confidentiality. Otherwise the details of your pending bankruptcy or your manuscript refuting *The Joy of Sex* may end up being tattled all over town. Please don't think I'm perpetuating a female stereotype here; my experience is that the human species *per se*, male and female, has a strong compulsion to talk about its members. So you must ask yourself, "Can I afford to have this particular bit of information known abroad?" If you absolutely cannot, then don't lay it on your lay therapist.

2. A second problem with the friend *cum* counselor is that she may lack the objectivity of a professional. Now on the one hand, that's a big plus in her favor: she really cares that your mother-in-law's weekend visit has stretched into three months and it may take a backhoe to get her out of the guest room. But on the other hand, without the grounding of an academic discipline behind her, her prescriptions may suffer their own mood swings. Watch out if she's a dabbler in self-help fads: into subliminal tapes one month, nude aura cleansing the next, and from there into Outward Bound Schools for Mid-Crisis sufferers. Depending on when you consult her and how easily led you are, you could end up on a three-day survival solo with two hundred dried apricots, a space blanket, and your same old neuroses plus a whole set of new phobias you never contemplated until you came on survival.

But the simple truth is that none of us would survive very long as a solo act without friends in whom to confide. Much of the pain we suffer in our professional and our personal lives is made bearable because we have one or more Someones who will listen, hold our hands, give a little common-sense advice, and send us back into the battle fortified by strokes, or feedback, or whatever euphemism you want to use. It ultimately translates as Love, and it works. It worked for centuries before Freud; it continues to work in the midst of the present crisis in the profession of psychoanalysis; and it will work in the decades ahead when we will be wearing our telephones on our wrists like watches and plugging into each other's home computers by long distance.

THIRTEEN

Luxury on a Shoestring

Who of us hasn't fantasized about what she'd do with a sudden inheritance? With all those giant lotteries, we keep seeing newspaper and TV shots of instant millionaires, all of whom swear the money won't change their lives a bit. Three days later, of course, the new yacht is anchored off Acapulco, and the only thing old blue-collar Bob hasn't changed is that lucky blue collar.

It is unlikely that many of us will come into a windfall like Bob's. But do you realize that for a very modest cost, for a mini-windfall (maybe a week's groceries or two), you can still buy yourself—well, not happiness surely, but convenience and even a modicum of luxury? And do not convenience and luxury contribute in their own way to happiness?

The point is that, for one reason or another, because of being reared by Depression babies or because of being Depression babies, because of genetic predisposition or whatever, many of us habitually make provision for just a little bit less of some things than we really need. (Not of all things. You can take it as axiomatic that you will always have ample zucchini.)

Let me illustrate. How many times around your house have

you heard the cry, "Where are the scissors?" The scissors. Because a great many of us—yes, even those with two cars in the garage and an RV taking root on the side lawn—have but one pair of scissors per household, usually Mother's "good" scissors, which are then always guiltily borrowed to cut clippings in the living room or asparagus in the kitchen or cord in the basement. People with stock portfolios out to here, and a computer room that could oversee the flight to Mars, seem never to have heard of "paper shears" or "kitchen shears," etc.

Let's get even simpler. "Where's the Scotch tape?" How long does it take you to find it? How much is your time worth? And just what would it cost to have a roll of Scotch tape in each major room? Maybe each minor room as well, if you have kids, because kids consume far more Scotch tape than they do vitamins and minerals.

In the interests of science, let's be candid. How old is your toothbrush? And could you put your hands on a couple of totally new toothbrushes in case someone got stranded at your house overnight? A minor detail, but odd, considering how much expense we will go to for guests in the way of food, beverages, entertainment, and other major items.

While we're in the bathroom, shall we just check the towels? I know people who have skimpy, limp little towels so thin you could spit through them—piled neatly right next to the five-figure hot tub *cum* Jacuzzi. Some day, pamper yourself and get some thick, luxurious towels that will make you feel sybaritic after each bath. You're worth it.

Drinking glasses. After my last promotion (and it probably will *be* my last promotion, but that's another matter), I decided that it was no longer necessary to drink out of recycled jelly glasses and Taco Time give-aways with Porky Pig cavorting on them. (Perversely, of course, the Disney glasses I had at the time I made this decision are surviving with a doggedness that is infuriating. Those two glasses have outlasted four cars. Honest truth. And I am not quite wanton enough yet to just throw them out. I always put them in the suicide slot in the dishwasher, though.)

But to return to the point: things people use regularly, like glasses and dishes and utensils, should provide a certain aesthetic pleasure. What good does your crystal do for your soul or your sense of beauty when it spends 360 days of the year out of sight in a closet? I've taken to using my crystal a lot—even for such mundane things as lunchtime tomato juice or suppertime Jell-O Parfait. I like it: it feels good to use beautiful things on a daily basis.

Stamps. How many times do you run to the post office for *a* stamp? Or at best, for enough stamps to send out the monthly bills, after which you are again out of stamps. Now I know the Post Office is threatening to up the cost of stamps again. But right after they do, I plan to buy twenty or thirty dollars worth and save myself all those trips and all that hassle for a while. It will be a source of quiet, yea, even smug satisfaction for me for months to come, to have those stamps on hand.

What price luxury? Less than you'd think, since like a lot of other things, luxury is in the eye of the beholder.

FOURTEEN

What Makes Botticelli Blush?

"A rose by any other name would smell as sweet," according to Juliet. But what did she know? She was only a fourteen-year-old who probably used her mother's make-up when she could get away with it.

The people who really know what's in a name are the pros of marketing. According to a book by a long-time insider at Revlon, most of any cosmetic company's big bucks go to the marketing division that season after season comes up with a palette of names for the product. Only a few pennies of what we shell out for lip, eye, cheek, and fingernail adornment go to cover the cost of ingredients: the rest is purely to pay for the enticement.

Take that rose Juliet mentioned. Of course no lipstick today would be called "Rose," any more than you can buy a tube called "Red." (I do remember a lipstick called "Windsor Rose," but that was a generation ago in another world altogether.) Blusher, nail polish, *et al.* are sometimes named after flowers, it's true, though increasingly less so, because flowers aren't, well, erotic enough. But you might see something called "Halcyon Hyacinth." Or "Tempestuous Tulip." Or "Violet Vibrancy."

But as I said, flowers don't yield many cosmetic names because they are simply too tame. After prowling through counter after counter displaying the make-up arts (this in Philadelphia's main department store), I concluded that any self-respecting cosmetic must bear a name that (a) hints none-too-subtlely of torrid passion, and (b) suggests food or (c) summons up the setting of an exotic jet-set playground. Notice that (a) is a must; (b) and (c) can spell each other off.

Now let's reflect a little more on (b). One might come up with several reasons why lip-gloss or blusher should bear the names of tropical fruit: "Pouting Papaya," "Mango Tango," "Melon Frost." I will leave those deeper implications to your fertile imaginations, and simply suggest that since the world of high fashion generally is trying to convince women that a touch of anorexia is in, the way occasional spells of fainting used to be, they can then turn around and play upon chronic starvation in the name of their products. Am I exaggerating? You've seen the come-ons: "Strawberry Sin," "Raspberry Rush," "Lemon Libido." For variety, liquid refreshment is included: "Daiquiri Dusk," "Marguerita Mist." As for jet-set settings, of course they abound: "St. Tropez Shame," "Acapulco Aura," "Maui Masquerade."

But above all, the lip-gloss we love, the blusher we buy, the nail polish we prefer must suggest s-e-x in the full spectrum, from light romance to heavy breathing. One line of cosmetics has out-done itself, I think. It has come up with a great name: "Botticelli Blush." What a heavy scent of suggestiveness there! To mind come all Botticelli's buxom, bare-breasted beauties, blushing or otherwise. And think what the name suggests by way of future possibilities: "Rubens Romp." "DaVinci Damask." "Goya Gilt." "Picasso Pique."

Ah, there's pure poetry in them thar' cosmetic counters. The product names will titillate, tempt, entice, and enchant. There's just one thing they won't do: tell you what color the stuff is. "What's in a name?" Everything but information, babe.

FIFTEEN

Avoiding the Close Shaves

Every once in a while, a little bit of pop culture among the male of the species catches my eye and invites comment. Such is the case with the current fad of Not Shaving.

Perhaps you've been too busy to notice, but it's become quite trendy of late for fashionable men to indulge in Not Shaving. We are not talking here about growing a beard or a moustache—that is an entirely different practice, followed, in my opinion, by a very different set of men. No, whatever Not Shaving is really all about (and I'll pass out my theories on that in a minute), it is definitely not about growing a beard.

Not Shaving means sporting facial hair of several days' growth as a regular habit—not just saying "To heck with it" on a Saturday or Sunday morning or while on vacation, as Johnny Carson recently did, showing up at the studio with a mini-beard after his holiday. Not Shaving clearly came into our fashionable culture via—what else?—the cinema. Way back in the thirties and forties, some movie heroes were photographed in the Not Shaven state to enhance their macho images. Chief among these were Humphrey Bogart, George Raft and a favorite of mine, John Garfield. Then of course there were whole squads of "bad guys" who presumably were instructed to show up for photo sessions somewhat less than closely shaven, from Edward G. Robinson to John Carradine (father of David and Keith).

Recently I began to notice that more and more movie and television buckos were "allowing" themselves to be caught by the camera in a pronouncedly hirsute condition. It began to look like more than happenstance. So while waiting in a doctor's office last week, I took notes from several of the magazines in the rack. May I cite just a few examples?

In *New York* magazine for last October, I saw a photograph of Alex Kimche, owner of new York City's Cafe Fidelio. He stood before an exquisitely set table displaying some of the house specialties. Kimche himself was neatly dressed in a fashionable dark striped shirt, a carefully trimmed short haircut, a sparkling white waiter's apron—and a Not Shaved face.

Esquire presented even more interesting material. On p. 48 there was an ad for "L'Homme," a product very carefully not labeled "cologne" but "a man's scent." In any case, the *homme* modeling for this ad was shown against a mountain backdrop, with his sleeves rolled up and his shirt open, most emphatically open, three buttons' worth. He was aggressively Not Shaven (though still without a beard, mind you). I guess if you're trying to sell "a man's scent," you have to really make a fuss about the macho business. Now on page 23 there was an ad for skiwear featuring Olympian Andy Mill in a beautiful parka, and Not Shaved. Well, outdoorsy and sportif, and all that, you say. But stay with us.

Next we have an ad for cigarettes: man and woman in a newspaper office, grinning broadly to each other in congratulations over having once more gotten the paper out. He is in slacks with suspenders and a pink shirt, only two buttons open, sleeves rolled, however. Lightly Not Shaved. All right—from here we go to an ad for 14-karat gold. The handsome model is in a very expensive suit, sleeves down and cuffed, in fact displaying 14K cuff links, no buttons unbuttoned, and more gold showing on finger ring and tie clasp. And his face? Right. A good two days' growth, maybe three. Millions for jewelry but not one cent for razor blades!

The crowning bit of evidence—still from the same issue of

Esquire—is a feature article on actor John Malkovich. Malkovich wears a jacket, a shirt with sleeves up and one button open, no tie—and a face that will surely win him the award for Most Thoroughly Not Shaven Actor of the year. The timing on this photograph must have been brilliant. Malkovich's facial hair is actually curling. Had the photographer shot the portrait forty minutes later, John would have had a beard, and that's against the rules.

Now as to the why of it all. First I thought it had to be a fairly profound cultural reason—the males, somewhat disoriented by the re-examination of roles that has taken place in the last decade, and concerned about the threat of putative wimpdom, have decided to flaunt the secondary sexual characteristics in an attempt to regain what they see as lost ground.

Then I wondered if it was a matter of males needing more territory in which to be faddish. Obviously, though male fashions do change, the swings are much less flagrant than the trends in women's clothes. There's only so much you can change in the basic suit-and-shirt, or levis-and-shirt outfit. And men's hairstyles, while more imaginative in recent years, really don't permit the range available to women.

But finally I wondered if maybe our brothers have reached the place many women reached some dozen years ago, when they tired of the whole make-up routine: liquid base, powder, eyebrows, eyeliner, mascara, eye shadow, blusher, etc. and etc. For a while, some of us gave up virtually all make-up. Today, if my observations are correct, women wear whatever feels right to them at the time, from a touch of eyebrow pencil to the full mufti. Maybe the boys just plain got sick and tired of the dictum that said, "Shave every day, and twice if you're going out."

Or maybe, just maybe, this fad is deeply symbolic of our ambivalent times—maybe we should ponder the message behind all those faces that are neither shaven nor bearded. What does it all mean?

SIXTEEN

Pocket Politics

The subject I want to bring before the sisterhood today is not a major issue such as equal pay for equal work or the right to have credit cards in our names. It is, admittedly, a smaller matter, but one with considerable significance in the long history of our upward climb towards justice. It deals with precisely where we are going to put that equal pay and those credit cards when we get them. In a word: Pockets.

Pockets may well be among the most liberating of humankind's inventions.

Just contrast the actions of a man and a woman writing a check—a small task repeated many times in the course of a month in our modern society. The man lightly lifts the lapel of his suit jacket a couple of inches away from his body, plucks from his handy inside pocket both checkbook and pen, and writes his draft. The whole transaction is a model of elegance, grace, and ease.

What happens to a woman who needs to write a check? To begin with, the check is in her handbag. Thus, she must find a place to rest her bag while she opens it—unless she has become adept at the one-handed zipper trick. She could also try to balance her handbag on her bosom, but depending on the size of both, she'll have minimal to zero luck with that maneuver. (Take my word for it.) Once the purse is open, she has to locate the checkbook or wallet-checkbook combination. She will pull out her appointment book (which is the same color), her address book, and her memo pad before dredging up the checkbook itself. Even then, her problems are not over. Does she leave the handbag open while writing the check? Well, why zip four times instead of twice? On the other hand, while she turns aside to write out "fifty-four and 32/100," someone may help himself to her Cross pen or other goodies lying unprotected in the gaping purse. And even if that possibility seems remote, does she really want others waiting at the check-out counter to be treated to the sight of the full panoply within? On the *other* hand, if she's getting change back from the check, she'll have to have access to her coin purse or the billfold section . . . What she usually ends up doing is jamming everything—checkbook, pen, bills, receipt and loose change—back in a wad, grabbing her groceries, and leaving with the handbag still yawning open and dribbling its contents as she goes.

'Tain't funny, McGee. Yet women's unliberated plight in this respect has long been the source of male jokes. The size and contents of handbags and abundance of other pieces of luggage that women traditionally carried evoked many guffaws and cartoon put-downs during the Victorian era—and the laughter goes on. In earlier stage and movie comedies, at least one woman would show up on the scene laden with huge handbag, needlework bag, parasol or umbrella, hat-bag, and shawl—not to mention shopping bundles. Often she would be trying to get in or out of a door, on or off a bus or tram. And if she were traveling on a train, easily a dozen other pieces would be added.

At a women's history conference in Minnesota I heard a fine paper analyzing the various items advertised as "women's luggage" in the Sears Roebuck catalog of 1910. More than fifty separate kinds of baggage were included, each with a distinct and different purpose, most of them unknown to us today, thanks be for small favors. The point is that even when travelling, women were and still are to a lesser degree laden with the trappings assigned to the keeper of the goods. The nineteenth-century woman was everywhere encumbered, anchored, and burdened. Women of our century are not out from under yet.

The answer to less burdensome handbags is, in part, pockets. Why do women not have pockets, and why should we want them? We want them because they are freeing. They free the hands, enabling us to stride through the world unfettered. With both hands free, we can pull open a heavy door with some grace and ease, instead of going through a vaudeville routine. We can grab a railing or swing onto a bus. We can catch ourselves more easily if we stumble; we can shake hands or embrace someone without a juggling act. Obviously the arms are meant to swing free as the human being walks, so as to provide grace and balance. What a fifteen-pound handbag does to that balance we all know too well.

Yes, we do need to throw out a good bit of what makes up those fifteen pounds. But then we need to have a few handy pockets for the rest. Without them, we earn an undeserved name for carelessness. For example, whenever I leave my office (which I do a dozen times a day), I lock it. Thus I must carry my keys. I usually carry a pen, because writing notes and memos and signatures, etc., is a continual part of my work. I often carry a couple of small pieces of memo paper. Now when I wear a suit jacket with pockets, these little items slip into a convenient repository and await my need. Few of my clothes have pockets, however. So I usually carry everything in my hand. (I refuse to walk around the corridors of my building carrying a purse.) When I use my hands, as I quite often do, I must put these items down some place. Then, if I become engaged in what I'm doing, if someone involves me in a conversation, if I start thinking about the next matter at hand—I return to the office minus keys, or the pen, or the notes. I am tired of looking for my keys! I am tired of putting down a good pen and then, when I miss it, spending twenty minutes hunting for it. I am tired of not having small change on me when I need it. I want equal pockets!

Now why do we not have pockets? Well, some would say that pockets, especially pockets that are used, bulge out and spoil the line of a skirt or dress. (The word "pocket" traces back to a Proto-Indo-European root referring to a whole range of items that could swell or be swollen.) But I wonder. I think having usable pockets, and especially putting one's hands in one's pockets, belongs to a category of behaviors, like whistling and sitting with legs outstretched—that society has labeled as "too casual" for women. Remember Jo in *Little Women*? When she would put her hands in her pockets and whistle, she scandalized her more "proper" sisters. But notice that whistling and pocketing her hands were natural, comfortable behaviors for Jo—she had to be brain-washed into the concept that they were "unladylike."

I wonder if putting one's hands in one's pockets may not be a subtle but clearly understood gesture of independence and cool detachment, the opposite of the over-burdened Victorian woman struggling to board the tram and rendered very nearly helpless with all her paraphernalia. No wonder men leaped to open doors for her! Walking unencumbered, with hands either free or comfortably in pockets, constitutes body language that society has traditionally considered "too cocky" for women. It is revealing to think a while about *why* casual, independent, or confident behavior was considered inappropriate.

Happily, involvement in active sports and outdoor activities have taught women in the past decades to value strenuous movement, comfortable clothes (shoes in particular), and confidence. And pockets. A visual stroll through the L. L. Bean catalog shows some of the handy places pockets turn up: in boots (knife pocket), in the back of windbreakers, at knee level in fisherman's pants and in overalls—well, you get the idea. Do you think we could push manufacturers on the subject? Working pockets for working women, or some rallying cry like that? I say working pockets because I've had too many close encounters with ornamental pockets that immediately fall to pieces from overuse—like holding a Kleenex or a paper clip.

Oh, and before anyone reminds me—I know that some men are now carrying purses, although of course their tongues would rot in their mouths before they called them purses. All I can say is that they're welcome to 'em!

Living Through the "Prime"

There are some things they don't tell you about the prime of life. (You can call it "middle age" if you want; I prefer "the prime.") Oh, they tell you about some of the little jolts. Who hasn't heard about hot flashes and bifocals? But they neglect to tell you about the age-group epidemic. Babies have colic, kids have chicken-pox, teens have acne, and those of us in the prime of life have—

Let me put it this way. Do you remember the Alan Alda movie *Four Seasons*? (It really was Alda's movie: he wrote, directed, and starred in it. Probably put the background music on the turntable at the appropriate moment during filming as well.) Now, who did I really identify with? Witty Carol Burnett? No. Volatile, feisty Rita ("I'm Italian!") Moreno? Nope. Skipping right over the blonde beauty played by Bess Armstrong, we come to compassionate, intense Alan Alda himself. But no, I didn't even identify with him. Actually, the only person in that whole cast who fascinated me (every one of the four times I've seen the picture) was Jack Weston, playing Danny, the resident hypochondriac. I hung on his funny, chilling speeches as if mesmer-

ized. It was as though he had eavesdropped on my phone con-
servations.

Can I establish some credibility here, first? Hypochondria
has not been a lifelong pattern. In grade school, I missed class
only when my rambling through the woods of New Jersey resulted in poison ivy so virulent that I was unable to talk through
my swollen lips. In high school, I was absent only when I
sluffed (to see *The Red Shoes* and *Cyrano de Bergerac*—talk about
terminal romanticism!) In college, if I cut early-morning classes,
it was because I had been up till 3 a.m. putting the daily school
paper to bed. In my first decade of college teaching, even when
I broke both ankles I missed only four days.

But since the prime began to loom before me—and before
my age-group peers, I might add—strange things have started
happening. *The Readers Digest*, stacked unavoidably before me
in the checkout line at the grocery store, shouts headlines about
a new disease every month. (The *Digest* is unfailingly cheerful,
I'll say that for them; the last title I glanced at raved, "New
Hope for the Dead!") But just that litany of diseases, month
after month, makes the *Digest's* optimism a little like the
mortician's.

Every time the doorbell rings, it's one of my neighbors collecting for the disease of the month. Last week, Mary Kay Peirce
came by soliciting donations for Snyde's Syndrome. I asked
about it, and discovered it's a rare disease of the hair that affects
only the second-born sons of Serbo-Croatian parents who are
left-handed. I gave five dollars. I know, my parents claimed
they were Welsh, but you can't be too careful.

Whenever I flip on TV, the picture invariably shows either a
live human heart beating away while six doctors perform a qua-
druple by-pass or a documentary explaining what a huge black
market there is for healthy human hearts and how many people have been showing up at the coroner's with an unexplain-
able cavity in their chests.

Telephone conversations with good friends take one of two
tacks: "Can You Top This?" or "What's Good For?" "Can You
Top This?" is a duet for alto and soprano, a melodramatic recital
of symptoms. "No, no, it didn't break the skin. But the rash has
been there for three days. And I can only raise my left arm
halfway over my head. Your knee is doing what? Did you say

your nose is aching? How can your nose ache, Gretchen? Do you mean your sinuses? Okay, okay, your nose, then." "What's Good For?" is based on the established truth that doctors, especially doctors who are not yet in the prime of life, don't know everything, right? And if we don't look out for ourselves, who will? "What's Good For" is the password to the underground pharmacological network. "That's right, two teaspoons of cayenne pepper, a tablespoon of honey, two mashed aspirin, a jigger of B&B, and a cup of boiling water. Well, all I know is that Frank's mother swears by it, and she never misses a day of golf." And now, after all these years and all the badmouthing about "old wives' tales," the guess-what-we've-discovered boys have come out and brazenly vindicated chicken soup and hot milk after all! Chicken soup is really supposed to do something for colds, and hot milk for insomnia. A two-hundred-thousand-dollar government grant some nice beardless youth got to prove what his mother and her sisters had known for nothing.

Your body will also pick this time to have its own identity crisis, let me warn you. You have eaten hamburgers since before the golden arches ever existed, correct? Suddenly, as you ease into the prime, you'll discover your stomach will no longer have anything to do with hamburgers. Or pizza after six p.m. Or cola drinks after twelve noon. Or serious, adult mustard a la Dijon, forcing you to the humiliation of sunshine-yellow sissy-mustard. Well, you get the picture; I'll draw a veil over the rest of the list.

Last night my sweet tooth was acting up. But sweets are bad, of course. I'd heard that sometimes eating a pickle will satisfy the craving for sugar. But just as I reached for a dill, I remembered that pickles are loaded with salt—very bad for blood pressure. What about a small chunk of cheese? Cholesterol. A little tuna fish? No, we're boycotting tuna because of the dolphins. Maybe I'll just have a slice of dry toast. What's that inside the toaster—asbestos?

EIGHTEEN

Sickbed Sidekicks

Let's be honest: there are worse things than having to take a day or two off work and stay in bed. Ordinarily, there are compensations, you must admit. But when you have a temperature of 102, you're in no shape to take advantage of the compensations. When I took my turn at the community flu recently, I was uncomfortable enough that I could neither read nor watch television, and for me, that's pretty bad.

By the third day, however, doom had mitigated to mild gloom, and I was even able to shuffle downstairs and respond to the mailman's thump on the door. He had a package from my book club. A package of assorted laughs, so it turned out. Actually, the fun began as I opened the cardboard box and tried to extricate the book from its protective styrofoam packaging. Roughly two thousand cashew-sized bits of styrofoam had built up a lot of static electricity on the long trip from Garden City; hence when I reached into the box to get the book, the little foam chips clung to my hands no matter what I did. In a few minutes, I looked like someone auditioning for a stand-up comedy slot at the Improv. I did five minutes of the sticky-fingers routine and found myself grinning at the waste of this perfectly executed schtick for an audience of none.

The book turned out to be Garrison Keillor's *Leaving Home.* May I recommend it for your next under-the-weather occasion. Except that the hardcover edition is a little large to manipulate while lying supine in bed, this book is a great companion for the ailing. Keillor doesn't demand anything of you; you can just lie there and be entertained. If you have a good imagination, you can almost hear his voice, and envision his lanky frame stretched out in a straight chair at your bedside while he gives you the latest news. The chapters of the book, originally Lake Wobegone monologues from the radio program, are just the right length: they hold your attention for fifteen or twenty minutes at a time (longer if you're an especially deliberate reader), getting your mind off your headache or scratchy throat, and then they're finished before you start to feel restless or prematurely well. And nicely scattered through the pages are various laughs, from little ones the size of very early peas to a few as large as a melon. In fact, I had to learn how to manage the laughs in my weakened condition. More than once, I started out with a feeble, flu-impaired heh-heh-heh, only to have it escalate without warning: hee-hee-hee-hee-ho-ho-ho-HO, a-ha-ha-HA-HA-Koff-Koff-hack-hack-BARK-BARK-BARK! All of this accompanied by the usual stage business of struggling to an upright position, searching for the cough syrup.

Yes, laughs are nicely therapeutic, taken in moderation. But that word "moderation" is important. Family members who have just finished giving a properly grave and only mildly embroidered medical report to your superiors at work and returned just moments ago from a drug store run, and who are even now preparing your supper tray—these loved ones are NOT likely to listen in benign silence to uncontrolled peals of laughter coming from your sickroom. Enjoy, but keep it *sotto voce.*

One more suggestion for those days that are less than prime: indulge yourself with whatever comfort foods the child within may ask for. Unless you had a particularly momentous tonsil operation, this is not likely to be ice cream or any calorie-laden sweet. For most of us, these "comfort foods" will be the items Mother produced to soothe us through childhood illnesses. I have one friend who is a gourmet cook: she makes marvelous pop-overs, exquisite French onion soup, and cheesecake that would unlock the gates of Paradise. And what does she want when she is sick? Campbell's chicken noodle soup. That's her comfort food because when she was a farm girl, Campbell's was a luxury, reserved for times of illness.

Another friend was taken aback when I offered her a glass of ginger ale one day. To her, ginger ale is still a special occasion beverage, permitted only when one's tummy goes awry. For another, the "comfort foods" are cinnamon toast and herb tea. For me, they are tapioca pudding and custard.

So if you wake up one morning and find that Type A (for Atrocious) Flu has come to pay a call at your house, hoist our good Prairie Home Companion Garrison Keillor aboard, brew up a cup of hot chocolate or whatever spells TLC to you, and ride it out.

NINETEEN

Sleepers Anonymous

I had my golden birthday recently—the big five-o. For some reason, birthdays don't depress me. I seem to have an oriental perspective on age—I consider each passing year as another notch on my belt (and of course, that may literally be true, but we won't talk about expansion here). I go around announcing my age the way other women in my actuarial group announce new grandchildren. That habit does not endear me to my old classmates, who resent my spilling the collective beans, but that's their problem.

I celebrated my birthday with three different parties. For one, I had asked guests not to bring any presents, but to bring cards of their own design or choosing if they liked. One friend tottered in with a computer scroll that was—this is serious, now— seventy-five yards long. Took half an hour to read and half an hour to roll back up.

It seems fitting to commemorate the half-century mark with such documents. So,

MANIFESTO AT FIFTY

I herewith declare my emancipation from other people's asceticism. Especially in regard to sleep. People in this culture seem to be in a perpetual contest to see who can sleep the least. I have many friends whose regular bedtime is 2:00 or 3:00 a.m. — which wouldn't be so objectionable if they were dancing or playing 21 or otherwise burning a party candle. But no, these folks are up in the night cleaning out basements for contributions to Goodwill Industries and baking zucchini pretzels. And these same folks boast of arising at unmentionable hours. When I was on a high-powered committee a while back, several women said to me on different occasions, "If you need to reach me, call any time before seven in the morning."

Look, may I be frank? I consider that kind of schedule in the same category as foot-binding. I have read (impelled by guilt, of course) many, many studies on the matter, indicating that most healthy adults, if left free of the bizarre restrictions of self-denial and nocturnal stay-upsmanship, will sleep between seven and eight hours a night. If nature has set our inner alarm clocks for an eight-hour tryst with the Sandman, what kind of masochism seeks to cut short the night?

Sleep is non-fattening. It produces no cholesterol. It doesn't pollute the atmosphere or consume the lungs. It doesn't result in hangovers or smashed vehicles.

So why the guilt? It used to be that if someone telephoned and found you a bit groggy at your end, she would say, apologetically, "Oh, I'm sorry. Were you sleeping?" The gaffe was hers, not yours. Now, if someone says, "Were you sleeping?" it usually comes through as an indictment, an accusation, and you have to tap-dance and say, "No, no, I've just got a frog in my throat, a touch of the croup. Who? Me? Sleep? How dare you even suggest such a thing?"

I know astonishingly few women who would allow themselves to spend an hour comfortably relaxing in a hammock (let alone sleeping in one). Now I'm going to crawl way out on a limb here, but I'll stick by my precarious position: I don't think the female sex will produce a great philosopher again until somebody learns the uses of a hammock, and idleness, and creative sleep.

One last study to ponder. Extensive research with people

who have had long, healthy lives—90 years plus—failed to come up with any constant common denominator. The very old include drinkers and non-drinkers, smokers and non-smokers, city folk and farmers, meat-eaters and vegetarians—on and on. No single constant. And then some researcher asked the right question. And by overwhelming numbers, the figures showed that virtually all of those who lived long and prospered had, throughout their entire lives, slept well and soundly for seven to eight hours.

So if you're on a 90-calorie diet and a four-hour sleep regime, look for applause elsewhere. And if you phone me and I sound newly-wakened, hang up softly. I'll recycle newspapers and use unleaded gas and conserve water and I'd never even consider buying anything made of animal fur, but folks, I'm going to keep regular hours with that healing old Sandman. And who knows—maybe by the time my next birthday flips up on the calendar, I'll be on some nationally televised talk show defending my controversial new book, *Sleep Without Guilt*.

TWENTY

Time Travel

Over the last few years, there have been reels and reels of films about time travel—have you noticed? "Back to the Future" is the most recent biggie, but there have been many others. It got so I couldn't even keep them straight—"Time after Time" and "The Time Bandits" and "The Time Machine" plus the others whose titles were not so immediately identifiable.

We saw Peggy Sue shoot back in time to the days before she got married. And in the best of the Star Trek movies to date, we watched Kirk & Crew boldly go, not to the farthest reaches of the galaxy, but to that bizarre frontier, present-day San Francisco. TV movies feature time travellers as well—"The Final Countdown" with Martin Sheen and Kirk Douglas and "The Philadelphia Experiment." In one low-budget but ambitious Twilight Zone quickie, a planeload of 1960's passengers got so badly warped they first saw dinosaurs out their windows and then, a few minutes later, the 1939 World's Fair.

And in addition to films, we see that the time-travel theme continues to be popular in literature—from a forgettable adolescent novel called *Hangin' Out with Ceci* to Marge Piercy's flawed but powerful feminist novel, *Woman on the Edge of Time*, in which a struggling contemporary woman makes repeated trips ahead to the future, including an alternate future when the luckiest women are pumped full of silicon and penned in expensive apartment prisons, playthings for the most affluent men.

I have a theory about our response to these time-travel operas, the movies in particular. Simply put, what we viewers most want to see is not the way we were (Streisand and Redford notwithstanding), nor even the way we may be, but the way we are. I submit that for most of us, the highlights of the time travel films come when we can see ourselves and our present world, as we might appear to an ancestor or a descendant. Time-travel films are in reality, then, not portholes onto the past or the future, as we might expect, but mirrors.

Think of "Back to the Future." Where does the film really click? Certainly not in the depiction of the plutonium-powered DeLorean car that is the means of the time-trick. And the plot is almost lost in the paraphernalia—we don't really care if Marty's wimpy father finds his courage. The fun in the movie is seeing the reaction of the 50's population to Marty's down vest, which they think of as a life-jacket, or to his request for "a Tab" (Counterman: "I can't give you a tab until you order something") or a Pepsi-Free ("If I give you a Pepsi, you're going to pay for it"). The smiles come in his mother's reaction to his underpants; she thinks his name is Calvin Klein because the words are printed inside the waistband of his shorts. The real mechanical wonder of the movie is not the magical car, but Marty's skateboard and his antics thereon. TV reruns and rock music—*as seen by those who never knew them*—these are what charm us: our own artifacts. We are enchanted anthropologists exploring our own dig, so to speak.

Although Marge Piercy's book does a much better than average job of detailing a possible Utopian future, a great part of the interest even here lies in the shocked response of the woman from the future to our present lifestyles: from cigarettes, which really terrify her, to sewage that pollutes the rivers, to our institutional treatment of the "mentally ill" which she had previously never believed, chalking it up to myth and historical distortion.

What do you remember from the film version of H. G. Wells's *The Time Machine*? For me, the interesting aspects focused on the Victorian gentleman's encounter with a liberated twentieth-century woman. A similar then-meets-now romantic theme shows up in "The Final Countdown" and in a TV movie featuring a 50's kid who comes back from death to teach an 80's nerd how to be cool. "Show the girls who's boss. Take charge, all the time." The nerd tries to update Mr. Cool, but without success. In all cases, the question is the same: How do they see us? How do we look from the outside?

It reminds me of college students whom I have frequently heard, in question-and-answer sessions with guest speakers brought from all corners of the world to lecture on their areas of expertise. Inevitably, the question is asked, "What do you think of Utah?" (Or BYU or the Mormons or whatever.) From Mark Twain to Madeline L'Engle, we listen politely to the visitor tell of his or her world, but what we're really interested in is us.

"Who is it that can tell me who I am?" King Lear asks sarcastically in the first act of his great play. By the third act, the question is asked in deadly seriousness. "Who do you think you are?" shouts Ruby Turpin, the self-satisfied hero of Flannery O'Connor's story "Revelation." The revelation she receives doesn't answer that question, but it does show Ruby, vividly and without equivocation, who she is.

So perhaps it should be no surprise that for all their gimmicks and technology, time travel movies satisfy us most when they hold a mirror up to our lives. More power to them to do so. Maybe soon we can move from watching outsiders marvel over aluminum cans and down vests and panty hose and skateboards to a deeper look at how our lives would seem to earlier or later generations, at what sociological and psychological shifts have taken place while we weren't looking. Such a view from the outside has an honored position in art; it's called perspective. The great Utah-born poet, May Swenson, begins a poem with these wise words: "Distance and a certain light make anything artistic;/ It doesn't matter what." Distance brings the perspective. And a certain light brings insight.

TWENTY-ONE

Women Warblers

A columnist for a Salt Lake City paper recently wrote a piece about my whistling. (Admittedly, columnists get hard up for subject matter.) Mainly, he was surprised at my skill. "After all," he wrote, "women don't whistle."

Now, the issue of women whistling or not whistling is hardly on the cutting edge of feminism. As the earth orbits the sun and our planet moves ever closer to the second millennium A.D., there are more significant matters facing us. Still . . .

In defense of long-time women warblers, I'm going to offer this column, not in rebuttal, but for equal consideration along with my colleague's remarks.

Let's get to the quick of the matter: my misguided friend said, "Women don't whistle." Now that is false. He had the evidence of his own ears to prove otherwise: he had heard me whistling. So the "don't" obviously doesn't mean "can't," as it might in the statement, "Dogs don't whistle."

As further evidence, I have before me as I write a clipping from the *Philadelphia Inquirer* of 15 July 1982. This item shows a photograph of an eight-month-old infant whistling, to the delight of the parents, Mr. and Mrs. Louis Cohen. The baby, you will not be surprised to learn, is a girl. Clearly girls and women can whistle. Whistling is not a sex-linked skill. (I have been told, however, by experts who devote their lives to the study of such oddities, that more females than males can curl their tongues into a circle. No one seems to know why.)

No, "can't" is not the issue here. "Shouldn't" is the real culprit. I had my showdown with this culprit before I wrote my age in two figures. Apparently, like the infant Carrie Cohen, I whistled precociously. I talked later than average and, alas, never learned to sing, but I whistled clearly and often from my crib. However, when I entered school, I first heard the couplet, so oft-cited to me now as to be definitely wearisome: "Whistling girls and crowing hens/ Are sure to come to no good ends." Crowing is the prerogative of roosters, and whistling is the prerogative of male humans. Women, says Society, should not whistle.

Now why has Society, in all its wisdom, decreed against whistling for women? That question brings us into the realm of larger issues. Some say that the patriarchy has long decreed silence to be Woman's best state. Women, like children, were best seen and not heard. Literature is filled with male narrators who extol a woman's beauty and lament its desecration as soon as she speaks. Oh yes.

A second explanation might be Society's nervousness whenever women showed too much vigor. Take more serious musical endeavors than whistling as an example. For years, women were discouraged from playing the visibly robust band and orchestra instruments—the trumpet, trombone, tuba, drums. Instead, they were guided towards more 'ladylike' choices: flute, harp, small strings, small woodwinds. It was this same brilliant reasoning that limited girls' basketball in my era to two dribbles at a time by any one player—and no crossing the center line.

I have yet a third theory about whistling and women. Whistling is a casual, nonchalant activity. It gives a message of relaxed, informal unconcern about anything but the present moment. In that way, it's a bit like putting your hands in your pockets as you stroll. To most of us, walking with hands in pockets is a masculine bit of body language—but have you ever asked yourself why?

Well, theory aside and despite Society, some women have always whistled. (I cannot give testimony about crowing hens.)

I'm sure I whistled so young because my grandmother, with whom we lived, filled her days with happy, busy whistling. While her hands worked away with a broom or pie dough or heavy iron, Nanny's lips trilled merrily, melodiously. Her music was the background music of my childhood. A number of women nesting up in my family tree were career women of one sort or another (mostly midwives and nurses, one store-keeper), but Nanny was exclusively domestic. In her traditional home I learned that whistling women meant coziness and good cheer. My mother whistled as well. When as a school child I was teasingly told the business about crowing hens *et al.*, I filed it away as more of the foolishness my father had warned me I would encounter in the world. (He often quoted Puck: "What fools these mortals be!")

Incidentally, though whistling is still in my mind associated with jaunty independence of spirit, I have learned that it is not incompatible with elegance. One of the most elegant women I ever knew was a colleague of patrician slimness, beautiful carriage, exquisite wardrobe—and wonderful whistle. For clarity, melodiousness, and repertoire, she was unparalleled. Nowadays, out in Nevada, they hold an annual National Whistlers' Contest—with prizes offered in both Women's and Men's Divisions. One of these fine days I'm going to polish up my rendition of the "Stars and Stripes Forever" or maybe "The Happy Wanderer" and hitch-hike over there, thumb up, the other hand in my pocket, and a song on my lips. Care to join me?

TWENTY-TWO

Peerless Pets

"Dogs' lives are too short," Agnes Sligh Turnbull once said. "Their only fault, really."

The theory used to be that people had pets as a hedge against loneliness. Well, that may be part of the truth, but only part. For one thing, most of the pet-owners I know personally are not the sort that spend lonely weekends playing Solitaire with Mitzi. They are more likely to be off on ski trips playing foolhardy with the buddies—but hauling in from the slopes every couple of hours to call and see if the nice man from next door is remembering that Mitzi doesn't like her water dish left in the sun. The cat-and-dog fanciers that I know are not the kind that gather moss and ivy at home with Boots curled up genteelly at their feet. They are, instead, out there rolling with the rest of the stones and trying to sneak Boots into the Chic Chalet Motel ($75 per single) while good old hyperactive Boots is wildly wiggling both ends against somebody's middle.

So why do we cherish pets? Here are some possibilities; see if they make sense to you:

1. Consistency. The problem with kids is that they don't stay kids. You just get to the point of mastering some child-

rearing techniques, and suddenly you have no child left to rear. You finally learn how to play a really good game of Get-Your-Nose, one guaranteed to reduce any tyke to a puddle of giggles, and whammo—no tyke. One day you start to initiate the game with your favorite partner, and this person gives you a polite, slightly appalled look that makes you want to hide behind the old *National Geographic*s in the basement. But animals! Animals will go on, year after year, responding with freshness and enthusiasm to the hoariest repertoire of antics. Why, I knew one old dog—and an uncommonly bright dog she was—who at seventeen was as thrilled with Get-Your-Nose as any diapered darling you can name. Now that's consistency!

2. More Consistency. Have you noticed today how people are always re-negotiating their relationships? A parent may think she has the upper hand with little Melanie now, but look out! Tomorrow is indeed another day, and little Mel will be maneuvering for her share of the power faster than you can say "training bra." Or take an opposite example: for years, Harry has been Numero Uno around the house—or at least everyone went along with that story. Now, suddenly in his own mid-life mix-up, Harry decides to emulate King Lear and give up the weighty duties of sovereignty, keeping only the rights thereunto appertaining. But you may not be ready for a new learner, having finally gotten the kids off your neck, back, hands and other segments of anatomy.

With animals, it's much simpler. Early in the relationship, in the milk-teeth days, one of you stakes out Head Wolf boundaries. And ever after, that's it. You won't be startled some chilly winter night by a request from King to re-negotiate your arrangement. If he outlasted you in puppyhood and established the final say, he will keep it until you put him under the daisies. On the other hand, I have known huge dogs to be perfectly submissive to a tiny child who simply never gave an inch. Happily, animals seem to skip menopause, the climacteric, mid-life crises and other human pickles. It's doubtful if they even have an adolescence—reason enough to love 'em.

3. Simplified Decision Making. Freedom of choice is a great boon of democracy and the free enterprise system, but, as you may have noticed, it can become a burden, for example during primary elections or while visiting Baskin-Robbins. What would Harry like for dinner tonight? For that matter, what would you

like? Decisions, decisions. Some of us are constantly replaying the classic scene from Paddy Chayefsky's *Marty*: "Whadda you wanna do tonight, Marty?" "I dunno, Angie. Whadda *you* wanna do?" Animals make it so much simpler. It may take you a while to discover that Puss likes milk-coated, fish-flavored Super Supper in a red bowl, but once you find that out, it's clear sailing, day after cloudless day. Clothes? Did you ever know a dog to set up a fuss because all the other dogs on the block had nylon collars and he still schlepped around in leather? As to "Where do you want to go tonight?"—for a dog there is only one "where": OUT. I tell you, you can get hooked fast on such simplicity.

4. Unabashed Pride. It's not considered terribly good manners to brag about your kids, at least in some circles. The fashion is to sigh, and blame MTV or the demise of the Great Books, or at the very least, the genes inherited from the Other Side. People who don't have children usually don't care to hear the details about Harry Junior's winning first place in the Make it Yourself With Plywood Contest. And if you start boasting to people who do have children, you're liable to discover that their kid came in second in the contest, which rather leaves you biting your lip and coughing a lot.

But people who have animals love to compare notes and swap stories. And somehow, bragging about your mastiff or your Siamese is not gauche the way bragging about your own flesh and blood is. I mean, after all, whatever else Bonsai, your feline, may have, she definitely does not have your genes. That really leaves you free to kvell.

I recall one conference I attended. At first not a single soul admitted having children. There were seventy-five women there, but the subject of offspring never came up, day after day. By the first weekend, however, the cat lovers had found each other and were whipping out pictures and comparing diets. Then the dog fanciers got into the act with more pictures and cute stories. From there, they (we—let's be honest) got into a great exchange of titles of books and calendars containing photographs of animals caught in the act of being adorable. Finally, by the end of the seminar, a few out-of-the-closet mothers elbowed their way in and defiantly slapped down photos of Tommy Jo or Heather, daring the rest of us to sneer, after all our carrying on.

Now, some of you may be thinking I'm ignoring one of the chief reasons people love and keep pets: because pets are so "loyal," and "they love you no matter what you do." Well, I'm sorry; as far as I'm concerned, that's just so much P.R. circulated by the Purina Company. Obviously I love animals, but let's be truthful. The only thing that stops animals from kvetching at us is that they can't talk. In fact, my mother swore that her dog Ginger "talked back" plenty of times. And don't deny that you have gotten some withering looks from animals. I'm not sure progress will do us much good, either; the folks who are teaching the apes to use American Sign Language say that the lovable primates are masters of the put-down. Anyone with a cat could have told you as much.

TWENTY-THREE

Liberating the Language

Bear with me on this, will you?
I've got to get it off my chest. I'm an English professor, yes, but stereotypes to the contrary, I'm not a crank about language, at least in terms of grammatical peculiarities that people expect teachers to be starchy about. I never say "It is I." I never worry about *who* v. *whom*. To boldly split an infinitive seems to me as natural and wholesome as it is to brazenly create fresh slang every half-generation or so.

BUT.

When certain groups of people fiddle around with the language for some fancy purpose of their own, I resist. At the moment, it's advertisers who are the cornsilk in my incisor.

Have you listened to the radio and TV commercials for clothing lately? In case you haven't, I'll give you the word: it's *pant*. Pants are no more; slacks are no more. For some unfathomable reason, clothiers today talk about "a fine wool pant," and "a handsome beltless slack." At first I thought this was just some oddball's peculiarity, but no, they all say it: "You'll love this pant." "Great price reduction on this slack."

If this change from pants (plural) to pant (singular) were

seeping up from the grass roots of the language, I guess I wouldn't object. But I can't believe it is. I can't believe that on a Monday morning, Harry leans over the banister and yells, "Alice, where's my grey pant?" I cannot believe that Bud stands at his closet door and calls, "Mom, is my new slack out of the dryer?"

What causes nonsensical changes like this? Is it somebody's idea of being trendy? Are we soon to hear advertisements for a scissor, a garden shear, a nice brass fireplace tong; will opticians sing the praises of their new bifocal or sunglass; will skiers be sporting a new goggle? It's to giggle.

Then we have the replacement of nouns with adjectives. There used to be an article of furniture called the china closet. No more. It's called a china. Look at the ads. Of course, it is *not* china, but does anyone care? Any day now, a bookshelf will be called a book. Only the copywriters know what we'll call those things we formerly called books. These same furniture dealers baldly tell you you can buy a dining room from them for $499.00. Of course, you couldn't put the studs up for that price. Their dining room is a table and four chairs. In the grocery stores, you see signs advertising picnics. The product being hawked is picnic hams. If you've lived or traveled in the East, you may have acquired a taste for Danish pastry. But in this age of familiarity, it's lost its surname: now it just goes by Danish.

The tinkering gets worse. Do you need face cream? Forget it. The least you can buy are some cosmetics—a word derived from *cosmos*, no less. We learned what the word meant—just in time to see it vanish. For a while we had "personal care products," which could mean anything from face cream to toilet paper and tampons. Now we have "systems." *Paul Mitchell Systems.* Does that phrase convey information? Not to me. It could mean anything from air conditioning to computers, but it actually means—cosmetics. Try your psychic powers on this one: *bath botanics.* What do you see? Large jungle plants taking over the plumbing? A rice paddy springing up between family ablutions? At minimum, a window full of flora, right? Wrong. Bath oil.

Mark Twain said that the difference between the right word and the almost right word was the difference between the lightning and the lightning bug. And Abraham Lincoln liked to ask folks, on occasion, how many legs a dog has if you call his tail a leg. If someone answered, "Five," Lincoln would rap out,

"Wrong! Calling a dog's tail a leg don't make it one." It sure don't, Abe: not in your day, not in ours.

Government, politics, the military (remember "disinformation"?), and, yes, I'm sorry to say, education seem as mired down in doublespeak as ever. Maybe it's naive to expect anything better from advertising. On the other hand, free enterprise has given us sports bras and disposable diapers: maybe the language, too, can be liberated. Don't give up the slack!

TWENTY-FOUR

Greeting Cards

Shopping for a greeting card recently, I realized that an anthropologist could do worse than study America's greeting cards for insight into our world of the Nineties.

For example, among other things that day, I was searching for several "Congratulations!" cards. Just simple cards to say Hoorah for accomplishments of the sort that need to be recognized by someone besides your mother. It was difficult to find generic cards, for some reason, but I did find a wide range of "Congratulations on Your Diet!" sentiments and a number of "Congratulations on Your Retirement!" cards. One might conclude that in this culture today, the two most laudatory achievements are not eating and not working.

Years ago I gave some thought to doing a book about letter writing. Three or four chapters emerged from these musings. Then procrastination set in, like rheumatism, and by the time I got back to the idea, lo and behold—people weren't writing letters anymore. Slowly but surely, letter writing as a regular part of life was passing from the American scene. Historian Carol Smith Rosenberg, who studied letters of eighteenth- and

nineteenth-century women, found that in the course of a lifetime they wrote, quite literally, thousands of epistles to family
and friends. One particular woman's output totalled 100,000 letters (admittedly, she was an invalid, and one can assume that
letter-writing was her hobby, or possibly her calling). Those
days are no more, of course.

Today, on the shelves of Osco and Hallmark, we find doz-
ens of elaborate, cute, contrite, and breezy ways of saying "Sorry
I Haven't Written." Now think about that for just a minute:
what does the abundance of such cards tell our hypothetical
anthropologist? First, that writing to distant friends (or more
accurately, keeping in contact with them) is important enough
in our culture that a whole sub-division of commercial production turns out ritualized apologies for the neglect of that duty.
And second, that even though the duty or responsibility is considered important, it must surely be honored more in the breach
than in the observance, otherwise why all the apology cards, in
all their varieties? If only a few of us neglected to write, those
cards would not be so numerous, nor such hot sellers. But there
are numerous varieties and they do continue to take up a lot of
space on the racks. It will be interesting to observe whether the
passage of time brings fewer such cards, as the very expectation
of letters evaporates, or more, as we find more and more ex-
cuses for writing less and less.

As letter writing has faded into quaintness (any day I expect to see it listed as a "folk art"), greeting cards have had to
become increasingly diversified and complex, to cover all the
bases formerly secured by letters. If you browse through a really well-stocked shop, you'll see cards expressing feelings that
in the past were vented only on the therapist's couch, if at all.
There are now several lines built solely on these serious, inti-
mate, erstwhile confidential topics. We could call the line Encounter Cards. "I know I said things that hurt you; you said
things that hurt me. Can we talk?" (The Joan Rivers special.) "I
was angry at the world. I took it out on you. I'm sorry." (The
Rambo special.) "You seem to have drifted out of my life—can
we reverse the tide?" (Owl and Pussycat special.) We have con-
fessions, repentances, confrontations, apologies, revelations —
all for seventy-five cents.

A lot of these encounter cards sound as if they could have
been written by Leo Buscaglia. (You know him: the huggy "Love

Doctor" with the beard, author of *Love, Bus Nine to Paradise,* etc.)
And that's okay by me—Leo's not profound, but neither is my
Golden Retriever, and they do many of the same things, thera-
peutically speaking. But if Leo is writing greeting card senti-
ments behind the scenes, I worry a bit about who's next: Ruth
Westheimer? Can you imagine what her cards might say?

I really have very mixed emotions about Encounter Cards.
On the one hand, the fact that people are saying such things as
"I'm confused," "I made a mistake and I'm sorry," "Let's not
drift apart," etc., is wonderful, whether they use greeting cards,
smoke signals, or billboards (yes, I've seen a few of those, too).
Moreover, I've been a card junkie since the old school days
when we got a paper doily stuck with library paste to a
construction-paper red heart on Valentine's Day.

All things considered, I'm for all cards, any cards; I wish
we had more occasions to celebrate with cards. I buy cards even
when I have no occasion to use them, just because I find them
interesting and who knows, I might run into someone who is
actually celebrating her fiftieth Mali gourd harvest, and then I'd
have the card ready.

On the other hand, too many aspects of our lives have been
taken over by professionals. In California, some people are actually hiring out to hold the hands and heed the last words of
people dying in institutions with no one of their own to God-
speed them on their way. In between, we hire women to have
babies for other women; we pay people to tell us how to furnish
our homes, arrange our closets, instruct us what colors we should
and should not wear. Gertrude Stein said it well: "Let me listen
to me instead of to them."

There is another development in greeting cards that I feel
less ambivalent about. These have wonderful drawings or photographs on the front, but inside—blank pages. Now that suggests a party game I would really favor: give everyone a beautiful or funny or far-out card and ten minutes in which to write
her own message on the inside to be delivered at once to someone else at the party.

When you care enough to send your very self.

TWENTY-FIVE

Camp Getaway

Remember when we used to ask ourselves what Americans would do with all the leisure time that technology would make available? Well, one answer seems to be that we are playing bigger and better games.

No, I'm not talking about Trivial Pursuit—I'm saving that for another day. Remember when you were a kid and you'd play make-believe fire-fighter? Or with a pilfered box of Band-aids and a bottle of colored water to represent iodine, you'd pretend to be a nurse? Now, it seems, we can go right on fantasizing clear into our Golden Years, if we want. The difference is that today there are people ready to give our make-believe a marvelous aura of reality.

Do you know, for example, that if you are a baseball buff and have daydreamed all your life about playing shortstop for the New York Yankees, you can actually do that? For a fee, of course. Each summer, the Yankees, the Cubs, and other major league teams operate a sort of Baseball Camp for wishful thinkers. For around $2,500, any man or woman can spend six weeks at the team's training camp, suited up in the famous pin-stripe, in the case of the Yanks, practicing the beloved sport, being coached by the actual coaches, and then, in the dream-come-true-to-end-all-dreams, play an exhibition game against the Real Team. So what if the final score is Professionals 35, Dreamers 3? You actually wore the glove and did your best to stop a Dave Winfield Texas Leaguer. You actually have a souvenir photograph of yourself standing beside Micky Mantle! (No, of course Mantle no longer plays, but he seems to be the popular favorite among campers wanting photographs.)

Now I think Baseball Camp for adults is a great idea. What I'm waiting for is a wider application of the idea. One extension—in which I am definitely not interested, I hasten to make clear—is already going nicely: it's a very serious version of every little boy's favorite, War. That's right. For several years now, grown men have been going off to War Camp and involving themselves in complicated games of hunt and track down, search and destroy, complete with guns (shooting what? rubber bullets? caps?) and intricate rules about when you're dead and when you're captured, etc. Apparently it really is a kick for some and well worth the several thou' it costs the campers. Ain't we got fun?

Well now, look: there are lots of us dreamers out here, lots of us high interest/low talent folks who would like to play make-believe for part of a summer. For example, do the people at the Metropolitan Opera realize their potential? There's that whole huge house not being used during the summer. I for one would delight in attending Opera Camp for a month or so—get a little much-needed voice coaching (if there's a masochist somewhere who would do that sort of thing), dress up in Brunhilda's costumes, strut across the stage, rehearse with James Levine, have my picture taken with (catch in the throat) Marilyn Horne.

Or let's talk about the really serious fantasizers: all those people who fill the shopping carts with Harlequin Romances and Avon Paperbacks and Silhouette Books. Surely somewhere there's an old Gothic mansion whose owner is having trouble paying the taxes and upkeep. What better idea than to open the mansion to a select group of Barbara Cartland addicts? Hire the appropriate staff—some sleek young men named Lance and Geoffrey and Quinton, a few Judith Anderson types for housekeepers and wicked-stepmother-stereotypes. Rig up the mansion with fitting effects and props—simulated thunderstorms, flickering lights, muffled screams down shadowy corridors. I'd suggest two or three basic scenarios from which romance campers could choose: the staff members could pretty much have their lines down; the campers could ad lib—with all that reading behind them, they know how things are supposed to go.

Oh, there are countless possibilities. I understand that NASA has numerous outdated space capsules lying around the back lot. Surely there would be takers for Astronaut Camp. And speaking of back lots, Hollywood must have many sets that stand idle for weeks on end. Who hasn't played Movie Star at one time or another? I tell you, there's a brand-new industry out there. Now that kids are going to school year-round what could make more sense than for parents to go to the camp of their choice? Be sure to write!

TWENTY-SIX

Family Status

In the mail the other day, I received a form to be filled out. It was from one of the growing number of organizations that keep tabs on me, and they wanted their files updated. In addition to name, address, teeth count, and other vital statistics, the form had one item that stopped me dead in mid-scribble, I must admit.

It read: FAMILY STATUS _____.

Of course we're all familiar with the "Marital Status" blank on forms—or even, on bureaucracy's off-days, "Martial Status." (To which I crisply reply, "Armed and ready!") There is an easy spectrum—single-married-widowed-divorced—to pick from for the "marital status" slot, though I'm not at all convinced that those four exhaust the possibilities. (I understand that on the West Coast now, some data sheets ask you to specify the name of "Spouse or Significant Other," abbreviated S.O.)

But how do you answer a question that wants a one-word response to "family status?" What do you say? "Intact?" "Dispersed?" "Eating me out of house and home?" How do you define your "status" in your family? Think of the possible answers there: "Still considered the baby of the family at 45."

90

"Barely tolerated." "One rung ahead of the dog, as nearly as I can tell."

Perhaps the question really means to ask about family make-up, such as who's in your family and why. If that's the question, they really need to provide more than a two-inch line for the response. I understand that the matter of who constitutes a family nearly shipwrecked the National Conference on Families earlier this year. One group kept talking about "the family?"; another group insisted that it was more appropriate to speak of "families," taking into account what varied assortments of people consider themselves families. Jane Howard, author of the best-selling book, *A Different Woman*, came out with a second book titled *Families*, which she might well have called *Different Families*. In it, she makes the point that today family groups are determined by many factors in addition to genealogy and biology. How do you define a family?

Especially around holiday time, that question, and how we answer it, can have a direct bearing on our day-to-day happiness and sense of well-being. Our cultural moorings are such that, whatever else happens at Christmas, we need to be with, or at least in contact with, the people we care most about and who care most about us. In a manner of speaking, to wrest Emily Dickinson's poem, one pine cone and a family can make a Christmas, but a lone individual plus the whole of Neiman-Marcus can still come up short. The key, then, is what we feel constitutes a family to add to the pine cone. I wonder if a great many people don't feel a vague but poignant sense of displacement during this season because we as a culture have had a limited sense of family. For so many decades, everything from the mannequins in store windows to characters in seasonal literature to the casts of TV dramas have portrayed The Family At Christmastime thus: Father, Mother, Son, Daughter, Dog, Cat. If the enterprise is really big-budget, the circle may expand to include Grandpa and Grandma and some extra kids. This image, repeated over and over since our childhood, convinces us that such a grouping is the framework we must have for that deep, undeniable need to belong and to be loved.

What is a family, anyway? Does every "real" family have children? Or can we rather say that the crucial feeling is one of connecting up with the on-going generations of the human race, feeling a part of the larger Family by holding or romping with those who are where we have been, who are coming up to where we are. Doesn't the belonging come through being involved, whether by blood or adoption or association or career or volunteer service or the most informal kind of neighborhood dynamics, with the next link in the chain? Some people who bear or beget children lack such a feeling; many without children have it nevertheless.

Is a family necessarily "incomplete" (or "broken" as we often callously call it) if there is one parent instead of two? The history of early Utah is a record of countless one-parent families, mothers raising large numbers of children with only occasional short visits from fathers shared with other families and with church duties. Sometimes these strong, nurturing pioneer families included aunts and sister-wives, live-in cousins, and children who became unequivocal family members not by birth or formal adoption but by simple love and need.

Gladys Aylsworth was a diminutive, barely educated English scullery maid who dreamed of a life's mission—teaching Christianity to the peoples of China. The story of how she made her dream come true is told in the book, *The Small Woman*, and in the film made from it, "The Inn of the Sixth Happiness." Human life being so teeming in that part of the world, there was little premium put on it, and babies, especially girls, were often abandoned on the roadside. During the war, Gladys shepherded more than a hundred such children across mountain passes to reach safety. A few of the hundreds of children she rescued during her years in China seemed marked, by some cosmic choice, as hers in a particular way. These stayed with her. She cared for them, saw that they were educated, loved them. Were she and they any less family because no common genes were shared, nor even a common racial background?

Some years ago, two young Southern women met as freshmen at a large Eastern university. Though one was nervously talkative and the other very nearly silent, both were shy and out of their element. They became friends and decided to share an apartment. Thirty-two years later, they have encouraged each other through career ups and downs, and through the coming and goings of various romances. They have pooled their savings to help Jill's nephew through college, and turned over their guest-room to Jean's invalid mother. Both teach Sunday School in the large Baptist church they attend. Christmases these years find them busy extending Southern hospitality to visiting nieces and nephews, cousins and other kin, plus university students who can't make it back to wherever home is for them.

A lot of people these days seem very nervous about what they call "the future of the American family," as though it might somehow become extinct, like the passenger pigeon. And I guess, theoretically, that could happen; I've read *Brave New World* and other science fiction that predicts such gloomy non-family and even anti-family civilizations. I've also read Marge Piercy's *Woman on the Edge of Time*, which fantasizes a wonderful, though different, kind of family structure. Yes, I know there are a lot of divorces. I also know that something like 85 percent of all divorced women and 95 percent of all divorced men remarry. And what about children? I'll bet if we did a count, we'd find that children hang around home for more years today than ever before. Eighty years ago, kids were done with school and out on their own by 14 or 16—well, at least the boys were. The girls were married and out on somebody else's own. Today parents are lucky if they can nudge the overgrown fledglings out of the nest before the boys start to go bald. And speaking of divorce, what happens when people do divorce? Where do they go? You guessed it. A good many of the women and quite a few of the men go back to their families of origin. And what's this myth about families carting their old folks off to the Home in their last years? Statistics indicate that only 4 percent of elderly Americans are institutionalized. The rest take care of themselves or are under the wing of a son or daughter.

Years ago, when our family moved from New Jersey to Arizona, our East Coast neighbors said, "But won't it be awful—Christmas without snow?" Our response at the time was to mumble something about the first Christmas not being exactly snowbound. But later, as we came to experience Christmas in the wide desert country, as we saw the delicate, lacy Palo Verde trees strung with hundreds of tiny outdoor bulbs, as we saw our Hispanic friends line the streets with flickering candles inside paper bags, making a bobbing chain of light and shadow, as we watched on Christmas Eve while the giant saguaro cactus, limbs upraised as though in benediction, became silhouetted against the darkening dome of sky, we understood: it wasn't the setting that made Christmas, but Christmas that made the setting. We hadn't loved Christmas because of the snow; we'd loved the snow because of Christmas.

So it is with families. Beyond the needs of basic comfort and safety, it doesn't matter whether a home is a hut or a hogan, or a mansion or a condo, only that within its walls we feel secure and cherished. It doesn't matter if the hand that pushes the stroller or the porch swing belongs to a man or a woman, only that it extends tenderness and an abundance of touching. It doesn't really matter if there's a big chair, a middle-sized chair, and a teeny-weeny chair, only that the people who sit in those chairs pull them around to face each other for hours of free, open-hearted, on-going talk.

Oh, by the way, about that question on the form that asked for my FAMILY STATUS. In the blank, after much deliberation, I wrote, ''Fine!''

TWENTY-SEVEN

Prowling the Classifieds

I like to read the classifieds. There's romance in those skinny columns. Sometimes when I'm feeling claustrophobic, I read the Want Ads and imagine how life would be as a long-distance trucker. Or I think what it would be like to simplify my life and become a Mother's Helper in some plush residence on Long Island ("Summer trips to Europe; knowledge of French helpful.").

Or else I browse through the pets department, like a child with the Christmas wish book, and mull over exotic choices like an Afghan vs. a saluki, weighing the unknown possibilities of a Burmese vs. the known delights of a blue Persian.

Of course the *New York Times Book Review* classified section is a world of its own. I'm getting good at deciphering, too. "DWJM"—that's classified for "divorced white Jewish male," and you can bet your dust jackets he's looking for "WJF—20-35, slim, good sense of humor, imaginative cook, able to speak several languages, interested in organic gardening; must be willing to relocate to small island in the Bering Straits." I like to project into the future and imagine slim, laughing Sylvia trying to coax turnips to grow above the Arctic Circle and translating Gide to well-fed Sydney by candlelight.

The other day, straying from the classifieds to commerical ads, I stumbled onto a service that promised to remake you from the ground up, as it were—clothes, make-up, hair, speech, personality. Actually, I got the impression that for a slight extra charge, they'd work backwards and upgrade your family tree.

But the line that really impressed me said: "Private closet inventory." Now I like that. To begin with, it has class. I mean, all the public closet inventories I've been to lately—well, to be frank, they've been a bit declassé. This firm obviously builds on a foundation of dignity. As I continued to mull the phrase over, I realized that I had never before considered calling for professional help in this area of my life, and of course, that's where I've gone so wrong. I mean, the days are past when we made our own clothes, permed our own hair, wrestled with our own income taxes—right? Why go through the agonies of a closet inventory without the help of an expert?

Now I understand why I have put this operation off so long. I know I wasn't equal to the task alone. I thought it was because I just didn't want to face what I'd find, but it's clear now that I'm lacking in basic closet inventory theory—I just don't know enough, and I'll be the first to admit it. For instance, I don't even know the statute of limitations on closeted goods. Is it true that if you haven't used it in a year, you should throw it out? Does that go for the marvelous Navy trunk I got at an auction in Massachusetts in 1970? I paid $7.50 for it, and it's solid brass and wood; you could explode dynamite inside and it wouldn't be any the worse for wear. Of course I can't lift it even when it's empty, but on the other hand, the last trunk I looked at in the store was $49.95 and made of styrofoam and Playdough. If I had a personal consultant, she could make a decision as to the disposal of my marvelous trunk.

And certainly she could tell me what to do about the purses with amputated handles, and the umbrellas with the fractured stays, or the divorced boots and the shoeboxes full of blurry snapshots. But I suspect what any self-respecting professional private closet eye wants to inventory is the wardrobe in my closets.

And at that point I gently but firmly close the door. Maybe self-help is the only way to go, after all.

TWENTY-EIGHT

Call Me Indian Summer

It happened in my local discount drugstore. I was prowling the aisles searching for some industrial-strength Porcelana, when I overheard two conspicuously well-groomed women talking by the cosmetics counter.

"Well," said one, "I used to think I was an Autumn, but then I found out that I was really Spring."

"Isn't that funny?" replied the other. "I've always been a Summer."

Of course I knew what they were talking about. I may be out of the mainstream as far as high fashion and new-tech make-up are concerned, but I still paddle around the edges of the river, and the ripples reach us all. These two shoppers were referring to a theory of clothes and make-up co-ordination that assigns each person a "seasonal" designation, depending, I assume, on one's basic skin tones, hair and eye color, and, for all I know, blood type and urine analysis. If you are an "Autumn," you look best in certain shades and textures, if a "Spring," you look better in others, and so forth.

Now my own method of wardrobe selection has nothing in common with matching up Nature's seasons and my own. My

97

categories are not Winter, Summer, Autumn, Spring, but Pass-
able, Shabby, Disgraceful, and Don't-insult-Goodwill-by-making-
the-offer. But I certainly don't pass judgment on those higher
up on the gracious-living ladder than I simply because their
standards are more esoteric. What I do question is the assump-
tion that seems to accompany this approach to dress and groom-
ing. The implication is that if you're an Autumn and you mis-
takenly or, Edith Head forbid, perversely, deck yourself out in
the hues of a Spring, you are subverting some master plan laid
before the foundations of the world, and nothing will possibly
go right in your life until you repent and get on the predestined
course. Haven't we pressures enough in life, without a new
creationist theory breathing down our décolletés and checking
the colors of our undergarments?

On the other hand, if there is anything at all to this concept, why stop with the four seasons? I mean, let's extend the
metaphor and use what's available.

For instance, I haven't the foggiest idea whether, according
to the ordained theory, I'm an Autumn, Winter, Spring, or Summer. (And please, don't tell me; I couldn't handle the responsibility of knowing.) But I do realize that frequently I am Monday
Morning. My face tells me, my body tells me, my mind, whatever segment of it responds to roll call, tells me in no uncertain
terms. Now an enterprising entrepreneur might be onto a good
thing if she put out a package of cosmetics labeled, "Monday
Morning." Nothing elaborate: a sturdy tube of Erase for the
dark circles, a packet of aspirin, high potency mouthwash, and
a small sign warning the outside world of your status. My own
sign would read, "Elouise Bell is CLOSED FOR REPAIRS."

On the other hand, I know a couple of people who are
clearly Saturday Night (besides Bette Midler). These women
wear false eyelashes, four-inch dangling ear-rings, and
see-through hostess skirts to change the Kitty Litter in the cat's
box. They look more dressed up going to bed than I did when
dining at Maxim's in Paris, borrowed fur and all. You can learn
a lot about human nature by watching the encounter of a Monday Morning and a Saturday Night when their desks are next to
each other in the office.

Very different from Saturday Night is Saturday Morning.
We all know a few Saturday Mornings, don't we? Instead of
sleeping-in like other mental-health-conscious folk, these

people are up arrogantly early, showered and shampooed and decked out in crisp sportswear that announces the morning's basic training: tennis or hiking, cross-country skiing, or a brisk fifteen-mile jog. And that's on Monday. You can imagine how unbearable these types are when it actually is Saturday.

Then there's Sunday Morning and Sunday Afternoon. If you think they're twins, think again. Sunday Morning is heels and panty-hose, a stylish go-to-meeting dress, and a sprinkling of "A Mighty Fortress" perfume. Sunday Afternoon (late Sunday Afternoon) is, quite simply, Monday Morning slouching in the wings.

And of course we know that some women are Mother's Day all year around. They wear big, self-advertising corsages at all times; the fact that the corsages are invisible doesn't keep anyone from seeing them.

I had an aunt once who was clearly Ground Hog's Day. She came out of her burrow periodically, but invariably saw a shadow of some sort (it obviously didn't matter whose) and went right back into seclusion again.

A friend in Logan is the Fourth of July—well, most of the time, anyway. In fact, her whole huge family is Fourth of July, except, I believe, for one of the younger boys, who apparently is Recess.

I needn't tell you about the people who are April 15. We all have a touch of that in us. I hear there's a new blusher out called "Livid" that would suit the April 15-ers to a 1040.

Phyllis Diller used to be a Halloween, but apparently she tired of that and changed her chemistry or something.

And then there are my niece and nephews: Hilary, Chris, David, and Timmy—each of them an undisputable Christmas, at least to these biased eyes.

The next time someone asks you what you are, forget about Taurus or Autumn: tell them you're Friday Afternoon and raring to go!

TWENTY-NINE

Power Napping

We have, over the years, paid attention (about as much and as seriously as the subject deserves) to the concept of power in women's lifestyles today. We've looked at the matter of "power dressing" (my suit can beat your suit), an upscale version of Dressing for Success. We've talked about "power telephoning" (whoever picks up her phone last wins), "power lunches" (my salad is classier than your salad), and even "power make-up" (try this blusher if you dare). And though we haven't examined it in this column, we certainly have all seen on the streets and roads and in the malls of our fair land the manifestations of "power walking"—a fitness alternative to jogging that lightens the stress of feet, ankles, and knees, and transfers it all to the shoulders.

Not wanting to be remiss in my coverage of power in its many forms, I think it's time to talk about power napping.

Bear in mind, then, that in the competitive business world, the word "power" suggests one-up-manship of some sort. Where napping is concerned, there are two ways to one-up the next person. The first is by seeming never to sleep, by staying at the office late at night to work and by being the first at the office in the morning, so that people will say "How does she DO it? Nobody can keep UP with her!" Since power, like beauty, is in the mind of the beholder, at this point you have power. Such a reputation gives you a definite psychological advantage. Three items are necessary to work this ploy: a DO NOT DISTURB sign, which you hang on your door when you come in at 7 a.m.; an inflatable air mattress, which you keep in your file cabinet and inflate as soon as you get in the office; and finally, a tape of two hours' worth of rapid-fire typing or computer noises or whatever sounds accompany whatever it is you do. Switch this tape on just before you lie down behind closed doors to get the sleep no one suspects you of getting. Just one caution: Be sure to turn the volume up on the tape recorder—to cover your snores.

Now for the second way to one-up the competition in the nap department. That is to make a big deal about how much sleep you get. Such an attitude brings to mind the old anecdote about the confident farm hand whose cryptic claim was "I can sleep when the wind blows." When a fierce windstorm finally came, the farm hand was found peacefully sleeping because all his chores were done, and all the necessary preparations for a storm had been made—all the hatches battened down, so to speak. This "sound sleeper" ploy is an especially good one if you live in places where the work ethic has reached obsessive proportions and people vie with each other to see who can be up first. If you boast about your nine hours of sleep plus naps and STILL get your work done beautifully, you'll drive your competitors crazy (which in itself gives you a psychological advantage).

You work this ploy just the reverse of the first: by coming in late and playing a tape of yourself snoring in the office, while actually spending many night hours keeping up on your work. You fall asleep in meetings—making sure you are caught at it— but not before arranging for a henchwoman to carefully take notes, so that after the meeting, which you apparently slept through, you can send detailed memos to people about specific items covered.

If you really want to mystify everyone, alternate these ploys from week to week!

THIRTY

Power Ploys

Here's an update on power ploys, if that sort of thing is crucial to your life-style.

I am still seeing the word "power" attached to a wide range of objects and behaviors in ways unforeseen by those of us whose competitive edges are less than razor-sharp. Of course the word makes sense in phrases like "power strategy," "power negotiations," and "power production." It becomes a bit more puzzling in its wider connotations: "power meetings," "power lunches," and "power dressing" (ties that intimidate; blouses that say 'I'm in charge but non-violent').

Actually, as I think about it, this approach to getting one up on your rivals, and those who even presume to think of being your rivals, is not all that new in my life. As early as the second grade, the power principle seemed to be in place. While most of us made do with a couple of standard pencils clutched in our nail-bitten little paws, there was always at least one classmate who intimidated the daylights out of the rest of us by something as simple as an accessory eraser that fitted over the top of the pencil—remember those pyramid shaped add-ons?—or as resplendent as a three-drawer pencil box with enough drafting tools to design Hoover Dam.

Power telephoning continues to enrich some lives—mostly those of stockholders in assorted phone-mongering corporations. The whole idea behind power phoning is to intimidate by giving a sense of the incredible busyness, complexity, and high-level networking that is your life. In the beginning, of course, the last word was the answering machine. That didn't last long. Today sixth-graders have their own answering machines.

Two or more phones on a single desk still carry some status, as does Call Waiting, the maddening little beep that lets someone put you on hold in order to take a higher priority message, most likely from a carpet cleaner whose truck is going to be in the area tomorrow . . .

The car phone is considerably upscale. The car phone says, "The world cannot possibly afford to lose contact with me even for the time it takes to drive across the valley." The problem with car-phone-power is that for best effect you must be seen phoning; anyone can *say* she is calling from her car. Last week driving along the freeway I saw a man in a convertible busily talking away on his phone and thereby blunting every competitive edge that whizzed by on Interstate-15. But as I watched him, a little inner voice said, "What's wrong with this picture?" I drove parallel to this captain of fortune for a while, and discovered that he didn't really have a cellular phone; he'd just detached the receiver from some spare set around the house and was happily talking to the breeze with this prop in hand. You must admit, his way is infinitely cheaper.

Coming up, of course, is the totally portable telephone, the phone that doesn't even need to plug into a car. (It works off the satellite system.) My brother has had a portable unit for some time, and likes to ring up clients in Saudi Arabia while trolling in Chesapeake Bay. (These phones currently cost in the neighborhood of three thousand dollars; if status is your quest, get one quickly before they start being hawked on late-night TV for $19.95.) Here again, you have the problem of convincing impact: how do they *know* you're calling from the middle of the ocean, or atop Machu Pichu, or astraddle the Great Wall of China? The solution is creative background sounds. Corral some Chinese-speaking students and have them talking even as you phone. Play an "Environments" tape of the ocean, complete with seagulls' cries and the dinging of a buoy. Dig up an old gong and claim it's the Tibetan monastery bell calling you to meditation. Your rival won't recover until you're made CEO.

Perhaps the most widely used power ploy is the appointment book. I can't even remember when we all started carrying these. Years ago, if we had a dentist appointment, we wrote a note in soap on the bathroom mirror and that was it, or perhaps we penciled a reminder on the calendar: "Aunt Blabby arrives Sun." Then suddenly, everyone in the world had a pocket agenda book. We all impressed the heck out of each other for a while, but then, as so often, overkill made the little purse appointment books banal.

Next stop: the four-pound Franklin Planner-Daytimer-Liferunner packages. These babies cost so much money they're apt to remain empty because you can't afford to go anyplace or do anything after you buy one! And there are so many instructions for using them (one comes with a three-cassette tape set of how-to's) that the main thing you write in the planner is: "Write in Planner."

Finally we move up to the agenda-on-computer—a software package that keeps track of everything—appointments, birthdays, tax deadlines, garbage collection days—on computer disk. It's a whiz: someone calls to invite you to lunch tomorrow. "Hold on," you say. You go downstairs to the computer room, get out the appropriate floppy disks, boot up your PC, call up the right file, type in the appointment, hit the save key, exit, store the disk, and run back upstairs to your caller, who, if she has any competitive edge at all, has hung up.

There is one power level above keeping your appointments on computer. Really powerful people don't make appointments at all; they simply say, "Call my office and see when I'm free." That's the ultimate. It's analogous to the desk situation. Middle management people have desks stacked high, suggesting that everything has to go through them, nothing gets done without their okay, they have their fingers on the pulse of the organization. But top executives have absolutely nothing on their desks, except possibly a picture in a silver frame, showing them posing with a marlin freshly hauled in at Acapulco.

Maybe that's what they mean by "less is more"!

THIRTY-ONE

Staying Green

O Tannenbaum! A tree by any other name would smell as paradoxical. Perhaps no tangible trapping of Christmas can equal the Tree in generating ambivalence.

To begin with, if you are genetically of the breed that observes Christmas at all, you must have a Tree. Many folks have wondered, in the privacy of their post-Thanksgiving picking on the turkey bones, if they couldn't merely forgo the Tree this year—just for a change, just to simplify things a bit. Well, those who have tried it report that it is, in fact, simpler to have the Tree in all its complexity than to explain, over and over again to all, why you don't have one. A certain affluent family of my acquaintance staunchly resisted being treed one Yule, only to discover, on Christmas Eve, a fully decorated Tree on their porch, along with a cardboard box of groceries and an assortment of dime-store toys for the children. Charity may never fail, but her eyesight can blur from time to time—especially if a Tree is not in sight.

Long-married couples who have finally nudged the last fledgling out of the nest sometimes think, "Now this year we don't need to have a Tree." Wrong. Word will spread quicker than spilled milk, from Fresno to Philadelphia—"The folks aren't having a Tree this year!" However inappropriate, pity will well up, then guilt—and before long, the good couple will have not only a donated Tree, but all of the chicks back in their laps, determined that the Folks won't have a lonely, Treeless holiday. Of course, all chicks will disperse before it is time to take down the Tree and vacuum up the needles.

Ambivalence lingers even in households quite dedicated to Trees. Take my friends Jean and Elayne. Jean likes big, full, bushy Trees, robust, hearty specimens whose vigor and pungency remind her of the forests deep on a starlit night. Elayne, for reasons known only to her analyst, always searches for a spindly little "orphan" of a Tree—one that she can rescue, bring in out of the cold, and turn into a Cinderella Princess with baubles and bangles and a veil of tinsel. After several years of unsatisfactory compromise (resulting in two martyrs where only one was needed), Jean and Elayne now solve their problem by alternating—one year a big Ethel Merman of a Tree that dominates not only the room but the house and most of the block; the next year a quirky little Meg Tilly that has to be coaxed to stand up straight in its metal base.

Friends Polly and Roger have a different ambivalence to deal with. They solved the problem of choosing a Tree some time ago: they bought a fine artificial model. But two years ago, Roger fumed amid a snarl of wires and bulbs, "I'm not going to put the lights on and off this Tree one more time!" So now, on New Year's Eve, Polly and Roger shroud their Tree—lights, decorations, and all—in a large green garbage bag and put the whole thing downstairs. The following year, they whip off the cover and behold—Instant Tree. Yes, the whole subject of the Tree is draped thick with ambivalence. Use the old decorations, worn ragged with tradition, or toss them all out and start fresh? Put the Tree up right after Thanksgiving and enjoy it all month, or spring it full-blown on the children on Christmas morn? Go the whole distance, with a Tree that scrapes the ceiling and crowds out the couch and two relatives, or prudently settle for one that perches atop the TV and seems forever an afterthought?

Well, maybe the tree is a compromise, after all, and a paradox. In the quiescent season of the year, at Winter Solstice, we bring into our homes the Tree that is ever green, to remind us of

106

spring's promise. In the darkest days, we light strings of colored bulbs and candles and fires to cheer ourselves and our neighbors on our way. These lights are not, after all, the summer sun, and the Tree, hauled down from Oregon or assembled in a factory in Taiwan, is not, after all, a crocus or a shimmering aspen alive on the hillside. But neither are we ever quite what we would like to be, ever quite what the promise said we could be. Yet that doesn't ultimately matter.

I think what matters is that we keep on, December after December, wrestling good-naturedly with the Tree, and that whether in observance of Christmas, or solstice, or Hannukah, or our own inner season, we keep on lighting candles amid the darkness.

THIRTY-TWO

Three for the Holidays

I.

Sensitivity training, conscious- ness raising, heightened awareness—I'm for all of them. But just for the record, may I say they do complicate holiday gift- giving.

I first noticed this phenomenon several decades ago when I joined the Mormon church and foreswore liquor and tobacco. Well, actually, I didn't have to foreswear them for myself, since the closest I'd come to liquor was the rum-sodden Christmas fruitcake made by our dorm mother, and my main consumption of tobacco consisted of breathing in the fumes of dorm-mates' cigarettes during all-night cram sessions for the Humanities 101 exam.

But in the years B.C. (before conversion), I always felt kindly towards liquor and tobacco for one simple reason: they were the only presents I could ever think of for my father, the only things I knew he liked and would use—short of his own schooner to sail down the Gulf of California and away from it all. In the years A.D. (you figure it out), I was never again able to buy him a present—for birthday, Christmas, Father's Day, St. David's Day (we're Welsh)—with any kind of confidence at all. Scruples cast a haze over the spirit of generosity then, and the fog has only thickened since.

My little niece came along a couple of years A.D., and she was a delight to buy for. She was a tiny, beautiful little creature, delicate of features and sweet of disposition. (She is still delicate and sweet, but since she has twice made me a great-aunt, causing me to put myself in the same musty pigeonhole as Dickens' Miss Haversham, I view her with a somewhat more jaundiced eye.) I bought her the frilliest pink dresses and the frothiest pink dolls and the cutest little Junior Miss mock make-up kits and the most cunning toy kitchen sets—and then it all came to a screeching halt. A decade after I got Religion, I got Feminist Consciousness. So much for pink dresses and frou-frou dolls. I don't think Carrie ever did figure out about the carpentry sets, the soccer ball, and the flowers I sent on the day she first started to menstruate.

I sent my parents, and selected other friends, boxes of Cummings chocolates for several years, until Mother made it quite clear that neither of them were eating sweets or chocolate at all any more. Another friend loved nothing better than a tender steak, so I sent him special gourmet Christmas boxes of Iowa filet—only to find out he had gone off red meat altogether and was starting to look squint-eyed at chicken.

You try it. Try Buying American, checking to make sure no endangered animal has given its life for your present, making sure the toys you buy for kids won't lodge in their throats or trigger latent criminal violence, double-checking to see that your gifts aren't sexist, Freudian, or sub-consciously hostile. Try not thinking about the forests that made the supreme sacrifice for your gift-wrapping; try ignoring the thought of the emaciated kids in Africa who could live a week on what that gift-wrapping costs.

I almost bought a piece of crystal the other day, a lovely sculpture of a cluster of grapes. Almost. Then the ghost of Cesar Chavez rose to haunt me, and I declined. Shopping takes longer and longer these days, doesn't it?

2.

You hear it every year. People inevitably bring it up. "The *real* holiday spirit." Do you have it? Have we got it? Where has it gone? Does anybody have it anymore, etc. I've come to dislike the phrase, and now I think I know why.

The problem isn't with the holidays; it's that word "real." I've noticed that that word is being used a lot these days, more and more often as a club, or at least as a barb.

Almost every group seems tempted to do an Us-and-Them polarization, and that word "real" lies at the heart—or heart-lessness—of the division. Real men don't do X,Y, or Z. Real women respond this way, or that. Group M aren't real Christians, no matter what they profess. In Israel, if I understand it correctly, some are claiming that Group J aren't real Jews.

In every profession, there are those who want to keep the blue-chip label for an exclusive few. LPNs aren't real nurses; Rogerians aren't real therapists; we even get instructions about who are real realtors—pardon me: Realtors. If some poor kid in the Schmidlap family messes up, some kinsman will be sure to say, "Well, he's not a real Schmidlap."

And the real holiday spirit? Well, C. S. Lewis wrote that the confirmed nature lover doesn't necessarily go searching for beautiful vistas and overlooks, but simply enjoys being in nature, whatever that nature is at the moment, that the nature-lover loves the totality, the richness of what Nature is, in all her variety. I suspect what most of us mean by the real holiday spirit is a feeling we once had under very particular circumstances, or a feeling we think we had, or a feeling other people tell us we ought to have, or have a right to, or something on that order.

For me, the real holiday spirit is the spirit that one is genuinely feeling at a given moment during the holidays. That feeling may be melancholy, nostalgia, joy, affection, longing, aspiration, mourning, joviality, kinship, disappointment, gratitude, grief, the whole lexicon. We expect the happier emotions to prevail during the holidays, and certainly we can rejoice when they do. But to say that the darker emotions have no place, are not also the real spirit of the occasion, is to reduce holidays, with their rich possibilities of complex personal and community ritual, myth, and archetype, to a scripted, one-dimensional TV sit-com.

3.

Dear Christiana,

Well, it's that time of year again. How's Claus holding up? Has he solved the union problems there? How did the affirmative action thing work out; have you had to build a new dorm for the women workers? (I understand they don't like the word "elves" any more.) I heard that some of the animal rights people were giving C. trouble about the teams, also. Thanks for the photo you sent in the Christmas card. Claus looks great— how much has he lost now? He's going to end up looking like the European branch of the family. You, of course, look marvelous as always.

As to my list this year, any or all of the following would be appreciated, old friend:

1. Moisture—rain, snow, whatever you've got. The trout in the Provo River need it, the watershed needs it, the ski industry needs it. Send it via native rainmaker, cloud-seeding, or the old-fashioned way, but send it.

2. Clean, invisible air. Last February was a real Valentine, dear heart. Can you manage it again? And the League of Women Voters have been such good little girls in Utah County; they may actually get the poisons out of our valley, so send them all something lovely. Maybe a class action suit, tailor-made.

3. A sense of priorities. Lots of people in this state seem eager to get certain books out of the schools, but precious few are concerned about getting books *into* the schools—textbooks, and the other luxuries, such as equipment, supplies, up-to-date office machines, and that ultimate luxury, teachers.

Guess that's it for this year, friend. Give my love to Claus and the staff. I'll leave the porch light burning on the Big Night, and some Wheat-Thins and Perrier by the fireplace. Stay warm up there, and stay well. We need you.

THIRTY-THREE

Chrismyths

The real meaning of Christmas. I predict we will hear that phrase almost as many times this year as the other standard: "Don't tell me the batteries are dead ALREADY?"

People talk a great deal each season about finding the real meaning of Christmas, but I think the phrase is a misnomer. Everybody who celebrates the holiday knows the meaning of Christmas, both theologically and culturally. What catches us up in a swirl of ambivalence and disappointment is something else. I suggest what we are looking for is the true feeling of Christmas.

There are a small handful of occasions for which our emotional responses are supposedly programmed in advance—like putting a ham in the microwave to turn on at a given hour, given temperature, for a given baking time. The arrival of a new baby, the Fourth of July, the wedding night—and especially Christmas; if we bring an unpredicted set of emotions to these occasions, we may do so at our peril.

No, I'm not going to talk about "holiday depression." Heaven knows it's real enough, but it's gotten so fashionable lately that talking about it is strictly *deja vu*. What I would like to look at are some myths that often get in the way of the true feeling of Christmas many of us hope to find.

You know how, when you're trimming the tree, you put your hand down into the ornament box and come up with a whole clutch of entangled, entwined metal ornament hangers, several of them jabbing you in the thumb as you grab? Christmas myths are the same sort of thing. Having become a slam-bang, do-or-die event, Christmas now has clustered and clumped around it a great many expectations, tail ends of hopes, cultural patterns, and for all we know, some Jungian dreams from our collective unconscious. Maybe by naming these myths, we can untangle the ornament box and get on with trimming our own particular tree.

The Myth of the Twelve Months of Christmas

Of course, it only *seems* twelve months long. But as far as our stress levels are concerned, Christmas begins the day after Halloween and ends the week-end after New Year's Day, by the time you calculate lead-in time and afterburn, or what writer Marie Shear aptly calls, "ancillary crap." That comes to more than a sixth of the year. Anything you invest that much time in should have a permanent end product, like a baby or 1000 bottles of canned tomatoes.

Listen: let's learn something from the athletes. Any good runner can tell you about peaking—working oneself up to the proper pitch of readiness, without cresting and crashing before the big event itself. How can you expect to experience real feelings of Christmas when you're sick of the season by Veteran's Day?

You don't have to do it that way, you know. You can wrench the fat catalogues ("wish books") out of the kids' hands and put them on the shelf until you're ready to take down specifics about sizes, colors, number of remote control units, and pre-scribed bodily functions of the doll-of-the-year. You can switch from commercial TV or radio stations (with their dogged "Dad Will Delight in His Own Caulking Gun This Year!") to PBS and classical music stations, or put on records of your choice. In short—you can keep Christmas out of your home until you're ready to give it the welcome you choose and it deserves. Whatever it is that seeps in under the door before the Halloween candy hardens is certainly not the real thing anyway; it's the crassest disguise.

The Myth of Good Will to All

Only Mother's Day carries with it more guilt than Christmas. Now don't get me wrong. The brightened faces that usually appear at holiday time, the little extra modicum of warmth and fellow-feeling shared between neighbors or co-workers or supermarket shoppers is one of the greatest benefits of the season. The problem comes with that word "all" in "good will to all."

Good will, we assume, begins with the family—parents and siblings and children and aunts and cousins and Uncle Tom Cobbleigh and all. But we're demanding an awful lot of ourselves if we expect to generate Christmas-tree warmth for all these folks on cue, especially when we may still be dealing with leftover ambivalences going back years or decades. But good will is expected to stretch further—to the neighbors and the co-workers and the people jamming the aisles with us in the supermarket. Then there are the Absent-But-Not-Forgotten. Depending on the kind of life you've lived and how much you get around, that could mean quite a passel of former roommates (not to mention former spouses), old service buddies, old missionary companions, departed neighbors now living in Boston and old friends now teaching in Beijing. But wait—what about those whose faces we don't actually know, but whose presence we sense? You know who I mean. The old folks at the nursing home who need visits, especially this time of year. The kids who need our quarters for shoes. The transients and other wanderers whom the Salvation Army's valiant soldiers feed and shelter. The struggling single mother with three little boys who needs a Sub for Santa.

Well, I've painted myself into a corner here, haven't I? Obviously I don't have a solution to the problem, but I'd like to offer a suggestion for each end of the dilemma.

First of all, at the narrow end of the spectrum—what we can do—remember it is the humanizing effect of charity that especially recommends it. If we consider charity, not mainly as a way of meeting the momentary needs of those who receive, but as a means of enlarging the souls of those who give (which surely must be its long-term objective), then a five-dollar gift thoughtfully selected and personally delivered to the widow, the orphan, the needy, accomplishes more in the end than a fifty-dollar check hastily mailed to some organized charity. The hectic pace of the season may allow us to take the latter course, but as food for the soul of either giver or receiver, it's pretty thin fare. Giving is one of the wonderful things about Christmas. The widow needs to give her mite; all of us do, however small it may be. We need to take it in our own sweaty little hand, and awkwardly, fumblingly, preserve that act in its essential humanity—the fewer frills or institutional interventions, the better.

Then, at the wide end of the spectrum—what we would like to do—we should be comforted to remember that what we are striving for is good will—not unqualified love or unflappable patience. Good will is a very human, very possible emotion. It does not require that we give without the means, or pretend an emotion we do not feel. Love cannot be manufactured, nor affection, nor warmth, nor intimacy where they are not felt, even within families. But good will simply requires that we wish our fellow beings well. In some complex situations, it may mean an earnest wish or prayer that a family tangle didn't exist, even though we know it does. It means offering up, on behalf of those whose material needs we can't meet, a prayer or hope or cosmic positive thought or however you do it, that those needs get taken care of. That may sound like a simplistic cop-out to you, but I have to go on record as believing that good will is ultimately tangible, and that those prayers or hopes or positive thoughts work their own miracles.

The Myth of the Enormous Potential

Charles Shultz has his Linus say at one point, "There is no heavier burden than a great potential." If true for Linus, how much truer for Christmas. Despite ourselves, we expect Christmas to be the highlight of the year. Our common sense tells us that it is unrealistic to expect our lives to peak each year on the 25th of December, regardless of what else has been happening to us, regardless of where our biorhythms are. It's asking a lot to funnel a year's worth of expectations into a cold, dark season that is sprinkled with flu virus and fuel bills, ice storms and overworked credit cards. We expect of ourselves, and maybe of others, all the achievements we haven't quite managed the rest of the year; cozy times with the immediate family, warm contact with the extended family, imaginative baking of fancy breads and the production of marvelous candies, attendance at a host of cultural events, from our 19th straight viewing of the grade school pageant of the Wise Men (which the child in my life insists on calling "Three's Company"), to the "Messiah" sing-along. Christmas is to be all things to all people. It's a little like the experience two friends of mine had. Just married, they were told by the bride's mother to be sure and call her when they opened their wedding presents, so she could come over, "and watch the expressions on their faces." Can you imagine a quicker kill-joy? Yet I fear we watch the expression on our own faces at Christmas, as well as on the faces of loved ones, to see if Christmas has lived up to its advance billing.

Certainly one of the marvels of Christmas is just that richness it offers. Assuming that each person responds to the religious implications of Christmas in her own way, let's look at the rest—familial, social, cultural, recreational, culinary—just for starters.

We somehow think we must have a four-star holiday in every respect, every year. I wonder if it would work if we chose more carefully the aspects we wanted to emphasize in a particular year. What if you decided that this was to be, for example, the culinary Christmas? You could go all out for the fancy breads and the peanut-butter fudge, for the brunch for a few friends you rarely see through the year and for a New Year's Eve supper that was really different. Other parts of the holiday could be scaled down: a smaller tree, a simplified card and gift list, a firm understanding with yourself that the world won't stop spinning if you don't go to every choral performance in the valley.

I remember one year when we decided to let'er rip—we were going to decorate the house to a fare-thee-well. We had pine boughs on the staircase bannister and an Advent calendar in the dining room, fancy candlesticks and imported tree decorations and frosted windows, Christmas tablecloths in the kitchen, Yule guest towels in the bathroom—and that was just as we were getting warmed up. It was wonderful. I loved every minute of it; I've never forgotten it; and I probably won't feel the need to do it again for ten years.

Some newspapers run a column during the holiday season for which the local citizenry provide articles titled "My Favorite Christmas." Now that's a nice idea; if nothing else, it gives us a chance to know the mayor or the governor or the mail carrier a little better. But quick now; can you name your favorite Christmas? A tiny poll I just conducted showed that eight out of eight people couldn't and probably felt bad that they couldn't. That's another part of the "potential" myth—we're supposed to have any number of Christmases vying with each other for Most-Popular-Yule laurels. Recently at a small party, someone asked people to tell what year of their lives they would relive if they had a choice. That led to a discussion of "favorite days." A lot of different occasions were summoned up from memory to show off their splendors—but none was a Christmas day. That doesn't say anything negative about Christmas, except that for most of us, the "great" days happen almost when we're not looking. Days preceded by a lot of heralding and horn-tooting and excess anticipation frequently stumble under the overload.

The Myth of Christmas Past

If someone from another planet just walked into the Christmas festivities cold, without any prior experience or expectations of the season, what would it seem like to her? Personally, I think someone with no experience would find Christmas absolutely enchanting. The problem with most of us is that, like old Jacob Marley in Dickens's "Christmas Carol," we drag around a chain, in this case forged from accumulated emotions of twenty or thirty or forty past Christmases. If our memories are good, the present Christmas can't possibly measure up. If our memories are less than good, then any present Christmas carries the onus of past failures, disappointments, loneliness, let-downs, guilt.

Most of us know enough to let kids be themselves. We know it's pretty stupid to say to a kid, "Your sister was always great in math," or "I hope you're not a troublemaker like your brother." Maybe we could transfer that wisdom and learn to take each Christmas as it comes and let it be itself, with its own delights and gifts and possibilities. This Christmas doesn't have to make up to us for any or all the shortcomings of previous holidays. It doesn't have to compete with some all-time championship season. This will be this Christmas—one of a kind, unique, with its very own shape and configuration, taking its substance from the shape of our lives at this particular point.

If we engage the holiday season openly, we stand a very good chance of experiencing that elusive "real feeling of Christmas." What is the feeling? I imagine it is different for all of us. Sometimes it is a large, splendid feeling; sometimes a small, quaint, inner feeling. Sometimes it comes in the midst of excited city crowds; other times in the hush of a snowfall reflecting the glitter of the stars. It comes now in communion with others, now in solitude. It can be pure joy, or delight, nostalgia or merriment, calm contentment, or glowing love. I would say we recognize the "true feeling" of a given Christmas by its genuineness and its mint condition. Gerard Manley Hopkins affirmed, "There lives the dearest freshness deep down things." I think we feel that we have had a "real" experience of Christmas when we sense, sometime, some place during the season, that blessed freshness, that newness or "renewedness" and vibrancy. It may only come for the space of a few chords of music, or as long as it takes a log to burn, for the duration of a hug or the span of a bob-sled's swoop. Its length may be a part of its preciousness. Somehow, a pearl the size of a grapefruit would lose something in the translation.

The Zen archery student is advised that she will hit the mark better if she aims less precisely. Joy can never spring to our loved ones' faces on demand; and true, fresh feelings of Christmas cannot be pursued like the absolutely perfect blue spruce tree. But in the richness and the sweetness (even the bittersweetness) that is Christmas, there do lie tiny, wondrous pearls.

THIRTY-FOUR

Counting the Milestones

What exactly is a decade? Of course we know it's ten years. But that is a man-made, a woman-made unit of time. Nature does not count in decades. Nature tallies time by the rising and setting of the sun, by the waxing and waning of the moon, by the budding and dropping of leaves. Nature may have larger units on its calendar as well, marked, for all we know, by the filling and draining of Lake Bonneville or by the advancing and retreating of glaciers.

No, it's not Mother Nature who makes a package of ten years and calls it a decade; it's we her children, with our ten handy fingers for on-board computing. We're so attached to counting off by tens we can barely make up a list that falls short. (When was the last time you saw a list of the Nine Best-Dressed Bag Ladies, or Eleven Ways to Use Up Left-over Caviar?) The very years of our lives we tick off in decades — my twenties, your thirties, her forties — even though psychologically, seven is apparently the more relevant number; (major changes seem to come, for many, about every seven years.)

But while we can look back on ten years and think of it as a unit, for most of us it's hard to look ahead a decade. Even our government, even the Russians, think in Five-Year Plans. Personally, we can look at our finances, for instance, and say, "Five years down the road, I want to be out of debt," or "In five years, I want to own my own home." (Some of us have more modest goals, of course: "In five years I want to have this dog house-broken.") For a woman whose formal education has been interrupted, five years is a hopeful unit: "In five years I could graduate," or "Even working full-time, in five years I could get my master's degree."

But even though we are the ones who create the concept "decade," ten years is, for most of us, too much of an hypothesis. We can certainly understand it abstractly, but it has few concrete moorings. Just what is a decade? How can we get our minds around that unit of time in a way as personal as day and night, a month, a season? How can we visualize the reality of ten years in a human life?

A former student drops by the office to say hello. Ten years ago she was a tall, gum-chewing enigma sliding in late to class, slouching in her back-row seat. Today, dressed for success and radiating easy authority, on the faculty at Harvard, she is much in demand around the country as a consultant and lecturer.

Another former student comes by. Ten years ago, he sat in class bedeviled by relentless acne and nervous fingers that twiddled pencils fifty minutes non-stop. Today he is holding a human heart in those now-steady hands, transplanting it, and with it the months, even the years, that it will bring to his patient. In ten years, we now have real reason to believe, we may be able to control the devastion of Alzheimer's disease. And of AIDS.

In ten years, starting from ground zero, I could learn to play a musical instrument—guitar, cello, flute, piano—with some facility and much pleasure. I really could.

In ten years, if you read a book a month, you could read all the truly great books in the English language; if you read a book a week, you would have inside your head the major masterpieces of Western literature.

Decades do get shorter, of course, as one's sojourn on the planet gets longer. If you're thirty, a decade represents one-third of your life, a sizable chunk. Since I'm fifty-plus, to me a decade is one-fifth of my experience. And at first glance, the changes brought by a decade seem less pronounced. Ten years ago it was 1980, which doesn't sound very different from today. But 1970, ah, that was another time altogether, a different country, a different generation, as different from today as it was from the funny time of 1960, which was still farther removed from 1950, a year accessible to me essentially because I *remember* remembering it, as though it were a movie I had seen many times, but nothing I had experienced first-hand.

No, one way you look at it, 1970-80 doesn't seem very long ago. To be frank, the seventies as a decade of American history don't seem to have a very distinct character to me. But as I ask myself why that is so, I realize it is because I have changed so much, because I was so busy charting my own transformations, that I didn't take much time to observe the transitions the outer world was making. Viewed from that perspective, 1970-80 is for me light years away. (C. S. Lewis once said that there was more difference between the average man in England in 1859 and in 1869 than there was between a man in 1858 and 1558. For Lewis, the year 1859, the year in which Darwin published *The Origin of Species*, was a major landmark in human experience.) Viewing myself from that perspective, I must honor the new cliche and say, indeed, "You've come a long way, baby."

And when I visualize the past ten years, what I see is the image of a road, on which I am traveling, in company with many other women. We are each making an individual journey; we each walk singly down that road, but we are intensely aware of each other. We smile at each other, we raise a hand in salute, we encourage each other over the difficult places. And we cheer together as we pass the milestones. As the milestones go by, it seems to me we are each more individual, more truly ourselves, than before, and at the same time, more truly together.

Hurrah for us! Hurrah for the milestones!

THIRTY-FIVE

It's Mine!

"It's mine, and I can do what I want with it."

Have you ever heard this defense of objectionable behavior? I think we hear it so often, spoken or tacitly assumed, that maybe we'd benefit by taking another look at the premise behind it. Among other things, a second look could help us understand some of the craziness of this past summer and "the old buffoons" who dominated it.

We first hear "It's mine!" in the nursery. "Mine!" is one of the earliest words children learn, and it's an emotionally laden word for them, as they struggle to develop that initial sense of self we all must have to survive as individuals. "Mine!" the toddler shouts, as he rips the eyes off his teddy bear. "Mine!" he insists, as someone tries to stop him from turning eight crayons into forty-eight fragments. And when he turns his attention to his live puppy (if his parents have been unwise enough to give him one), it takes quite an effort to teach him that "Mine!" doesn't mean he can pull the creature's tail, squeeze the breath out of him, or run him through the clothes dryer.

When that toddler shoots up another few feet and gets his

first car, he'll learn more about restrictions on what is "his." He may have paid for that car with buckets of sweat, but there are very particular limits on how he can drive it, park it, maintain it, license it, sell it, or junk it. And the restrictions swell to a whole series of code books when he buys real estate. "It's mine" may be true, but that corollary—"and I can do what I want with it"—becomes less and less valid as the world's population grows, and with it, our sense of responsibility for and to each other.

In America, and especially here in the West, the traditional laissez faire idea dies hard.

Freedom means much to us. In the past, whenever civilization breathed too hot down a person's neck, he (rarely she) could pack up, ride west for a day or a week or a month, stake out a claim on some uncivilized land, and do pretty much anything with and on that land. For better or worse, those days are no more. Of course, we're still arguing about whether we're free to slash all the timber off a mountainside to make toilet paper, dump toxic wastes in our lakes and streams, shoot coyotes, restrict access to wilderness, and a hundred other particulars. But most of us share the premise that we are not free to do whatever we want with this planet, because it is "ours" only in a carefully defined sense of that word.

(As a small example, the Mormon leadership has recently discovered that even though they can validly say "It's ours" about the Hotel Utah, many citizens disagree about the corollary: "We can do what we want with it." Some people seem to feel that, as in the case of the Coalville Tabernacle and other landmarks, once a building has become part of the community, participating and benefitting from the give and take of community life, there is then a shared right as well as a shared responsibility.)

"She's mine," husbands have said about wives for centuries, and for all but a tiny recent slice of that time, the law upheld them. Women were chattel, and so were children. Beat them, rape them, work them till they dropped in the mines or the mills or the fields; the defense was recognized—"They're mine, and I can do what I want with them." We're working on cleaning up the ragged edges of that problem today, on issues such as marital rape, all forms of child abuse, and a whole range of more subtle questions: Must your daughter have your permission before she can get birth control pills? Can the state force you to send your son to a public school? To innoculate him against contagious diseases? If your baby is ill in the hospital, can you be forced to allow a blood transfusion, even against your principles? If your newborn suffers from multiple birth defects, will you be allowed to turn off life support systems? A man's salary may be his, but in Michigan, for example, the state can now take money out of his paycheck to cover child support.

How does all this relate to Oliver North and Ronald Reagan and the rest of the "Rough Riders" involved in the messy Iran-Contra Affair?

It occurs to me that if we say "mine!" so adamantly about teddy bears and tricycles, property and even other people, we also say it with equal passion about our positions, our jobs and the status that goes with them. People have confused themselves with their jobs long before Louis xiv said, *"L'état, c'est moi!"* Look around you. Don't you know a manager or a mother, a bishop or a dean or a dad who has so thoroughly blurred the lines that the job has become the identity? Such people come to believe that whatever they want, whatever they think best for the institution—that *is* best. No one knows the whole story better than they, no one loves the institution more, and any who think otherwise are enemies to be outwitted.

Perhaps the most dramatic example of such merging of person and position in this century was J. Edgar Hoover, founder and first director of the FBI. Hoover *was* the FBI for decades. Presidents came and went, but Hoover stayed. No wonder that he felt himself accountable only to God. Hoover left a great legacy, but the record shows his sense of sovereignty also resulted in serious abuses. The bureau wasn't ours; it was his.

He could do what he liked with it. The fabric of democracy starts to unravel when people believe that way.

And so we come to Oliver North, happily offering himself as the fall guy, the shield between his superiors ("Us") and Congress, the Justice Department, and the American public ("Them"). We come to Admiral John Poindexter, the president's "National Security Advisor," stoically puffing his pipe, ready to go down with his ship, and totally convinced to the end that it is, indeed, his ship. And we come to the Big Guy, Ronald Reagan. Nationally syndicated columnist James Reston has pointed out that every president in this century who won a second term by a large margin has been involved in a major scandal during that second term. Apparently it is far too easy to move from the premise, "The people support what I'm doing" to the conclusion "Whatever I do, the people will support." We all know that power can corrupt us, wherever we exercise it, and that for that reason it must be handled as are all powerful, dangerous things. But it is only absolute power that corrupts absolutely, as Lord Acton said—absolute power, the power that thinks it must answer to no one, that power that shouts, "Mine! And I can do with it what I like!"

THIRTY-SIX

A Fable for Our Time

Once upon a time (upon several times, actually), a fair young maiden sat weeping in a corner of her kitchen. Everyone else was going to a party, but Kate had nothing to wear, and instead was forced by her wicked step-conscience to stay at home and feed vegetables to the Cuisinart for tomorrow's dinner.

"Oh why couldn't I have just one pair of jeans?" she moaned. "Nothing but Laura Ashleys and certified Dress-For-Success suits! Wouldn't they be laughable at this event? Oh, woe is me! I wish—I wish—"

Suddenly there was a blinding flash of light, followed by darkness.

"Drat!" said Kate. "I knew this Cuisinart would overload the circuits!"

But as suddenly as it had come, the darkness left. And at her kitchen table sat a woman Kate had never seen before. Even in the middle of her surprise, Kate noticed that she was dressed perfectly for the party—cool white slacks and a shirt in the most wonderful shades of blue and lavender all running together like the aftermath of a spring shower. Her dark blonde hair hung down her back in a thick French braid. She looked like a cross between a young Ingrid Bergman and a mature Marietta Hartley, with something of Sharon Gless around the mouth. Kate had a moment of annoyance to think that even a Power & Light worker had a better, a more comprehensive wardrobe than she did.

"Yes?" said the woman, which seemed more like Kate's line.

"Uh, well, yes, I guess I shouldn't have plugged in the food processor while the printer was still running but I—"

"The circuitry is fine," said the woman. "What is it you wish?"

"What?"

The woman consulted the Franklin Planner open on the table before her. Then she read off, in the voice of a court recorder, "Saturday the 25th, nine-oh-two p.m. 'Oh woe is me! I wish—I wish—.' Well, Kate, I am Miranda Verasdaughter, F.G., and I am here to grant your wish. In fact, you have been alloted—" (another quick glance into the Planner) "yes, three wishes. Will you sign right here—bottom line, where the X is." She held out a small clipboard, with a form in tri-color triplicate attached.

"I know!" Kate said suddenly. "I'll bet you're from Western Onion, aren't you? This is from the gang at the party, isn't it? Are you going to sing something? Are there balloons with this?"

The woman laid a cool, gentle hand on Kate's arm.

"I wish I could stay and philosophize, Kate. But I can't. You'll just have to figure this out on your own. Read the bottom line." The look in her blue eyes compelled Kate to sign the form and to take the offered pink copy.

"Good-bye, Kate," said Miranda. "Enjoy."

Just then the Cuisinart starting screeching and grinding, building to an absolute crescendo of agony. Kate turned to silence it. When she turned back, Miranda had vanished.

Kate spent the rest of the evening trying to figure out who was behind the joke. It was a cute gag, but actually, she didn't know anybody with the energy—or frankly, the interest—to go to that kind of trouble to give her a laugh.

After she had studied the pink receipt for the tenth time, she happened to turn it over. The back was a thicket of very very fine print. It was not a legal contract; it seemed to be a biography of her life right up to the moment the food processor had started misbehaving, and it had many precise and private details, so many that Kate at one point stopped reading and whispered, "FBI!" But even with chronic paranoia, she knew that was absurd. Besides, some of these things, even the FBI couldn't know, because they had never been spoken or written to anyone, but were the secret hoardings of her heart. Two of them she had never even acknowledged to herself, and knew to be the truth only in the moment she read them.

Whatever it was, this was no gag. That night, in a dream, Miranda returned to her. She took Kate's face in her hands, looked steadily into her eyes, and said, "Get on with it!"

Now Kate was not your typical foolish young maiden. Don't look for her to waste her three wishes on trivial whims or unthinking inanities: "I wish there were something decent on TV"; "I wish I knew what to do with my hair," etc. No indeed! (She was a Virgo, after all.)

"I probably shouldn't make any decision at all for a long time—the way they tell you to do when a spouse dies." So she locked the pink receipt in her safety deposit box for a full calendar year.

During that year, of course, she thought a great deal. And she worked on herself to avoid any inadvertent slips. In fact, she totally exiled the word "wish" from her vocabulary. She never said, "Oh, thanks, I wish I could go but I can't." Or "I wish this heat would break." Or "I wish" anything.

She knew that, according to folklore, the three-wishes scenario is fraught with irony. Even O. Henry knew that: boy wishes for fancy watch-fob for his fine watch, girl wishes for fancy combs for her long hair. Boy sells watch to buy combs for girl, who has cut and sold her hair to buy watch-fob. Couple wishes for money; it comes in the form of insurance upon the death of their beloved son. They wish for him back, and a grisly corpse begins thumping on the door. Etc.

There had to be some catch involved with this . . . offer. (Actually, she had taken to thinking of it as a grant. It seemed easier to deal with that way.) She needed to be very careful and examine all potential snags before committing herself. She wasn't going to race around any blind curve in the road before knowing what lay ahead.

But there was a greater problem. What did she really want? Oh, she wanted a lot of things, of course. But what did she really *want*?

The second year, her apartment filled up with catalogs and pamphlets and brochures. Neiman-Marcus and Spiegel, Thomasville and Lladro. Arabian Nights Tours and Joy Lake Personal Growth Seminars. A steady stream of "agents" called on her. She saw slide presentations about land in New Mexico and Colorado; she spent complimentary weekends at condo developments on Oahu and in Vermont. She test-drove BMWs, Porsches, a Bentley.

During the third year, Miranda came to her frequently in dreams, but only for the briefest moments. One night Kate fell wearily into bed (she no longer slept well) thinking, "Wishing never made anything happen." Miranda appeared that night, a face on a TV commercial, and said, "Nothing ever happened without wishing." Another night, Kate wrestled with the idea that people should *struggle* for what they want in life. This time she saw Miranda driving a creamy convertible with a bumper sticker that read: STRUGGLE IS HIGHLY OVER-RATED. ESPECIALLY AS A LIFESTYLE. In the middle of that winter, an especially cold and dreary winter, Kate fretted for a week, convinced that if she were granted three wishes, no matter what she asked for, she would be changed, become a different person. In that night's dream, she cracked open a fortune cookie and read, "YOU WILL CHANGE IN ANY CASE."

In the fourth year, she became a cynic. Any wish that came to her mind immediately triggered a scenario of disappointment, disillusionment, and emptiness amid splendor. Her Cuisinart broke down completely; she never got it fixed.

The fifth year she writhed in an agony of unworthiness. Who was she to have her wishes answered, when the world tottered in pain, hunger, and want? She devoured newspapers that year, choking down accounts of pestilence and famine, wars and fires and earthquakes; toddlers needing transplants; wildlife societies begging for help to save the whales, the seals, the tigers, the rhinos, the snail darters; the homeless clogging the streets of every major metropolis as the smog once did; street children infesting the thoroughfares of Rio and Buenos Aires and Cairo and Calcutta, the weak ones dying, the strong ones surviving to perpetuate lives of fierce theft, deception, expediency, grief. Three wishes against all that?

Eleven o'clock on New Year's Eve of the fifth year, Kate was alone in her apartment, drinking her second bottle of white wine. She couldn't stand to have the TV on; she couldn't stand to have it off. She compromised: picture, but no sound. Suddenly, the sound came on, unasked for.

"Kate." It was Miranda. "Kate, I'm sorry to say this. We are rescinding your . . . 'grant.' "

Kate wasn't surprised.

"I guess there are only so many wishes to go around, hum? Well, I understand."

"You don't, Kate; that's the problem. Did you ever read the bottom line on your contract?" The pink receipt was still in the safety deposit box. On the TV screen, Miranda flashed a yellow copy of the form, greatly enlarged. Kate read, "RENEWABLE IN PERPETUITY."

"Now wait a minute—"

"We've waited five years, Kate. The wishes are renewable. Three wishes are only the start. You could follow that with nine, and eighty-one, and 6,561—"

"If that's so, if there's enough to go around and then some, why are you rescinding?"

"Abundance is encouraged; waste is not. Every wish is made up of universal energy. You've locked yours up, instead of recycling it. A tragic waste. But never mind, Kate! There's still time. You have twenty minutes before midnight, when the contract lapses. Take them now! Take all three wishes!" There was that Sharon Gless insistence in Miranda's eyes, the Ingrid Bergman urgency in her voice.

"What—now? Just like that?" And her brain fuddled with two bottles of wine, she almost added.

"Do it!"

Something seemed to happen to all the appliances in the place. The hum of the fridge grew palpable. She swore she could hear the electricity zapping in the wires behind the walls. The forced air heating breathed out swirls of invisible fog. Miranda's voice sounded far, far away, though Kate could hear every word.

"This is the only moment there is. Put out your hand, Kate. In the beginning is always the word. Say it!"

"I wish—I wish—"

Somebody from Times Square was counting down: "10-9-8 . . ."

Horns and whistles and screams filled the background. (But the sound was turned all the way down on the TV.)

"I WISH I KNEW WHAT TO WISH FOR!"

At that moment, the fifth dimension unfolded. Kate's brain became the sixth. The seventh dimension blossomed like a time-lapsed flower. The eighth and ninth billowed out together, mirror images. The tenth and the eleventh . . .

Miranda's laughter floated joyous through them all.